Beowulf
&
Beyond

Beowulf & Beyond

Copyright © 2021 by Dan Veach

All rights reserved. No part of this work may be reproduced or transmitted in any form or by any means, electronic or mechanical, including photocopying and recording, or by means of any information storage or retrieval system, except as may be expressly permitted by the 1976 Copyright Act or in writing from the publisher. Requests for permission should be addressed in writing to Lockwood Press, PO Box 133289, Atlanta, GA 30333 USA.

ISBN: 978-1-948488-61-7

Cover design by Susanne Wilhelm.

Cover image: Shoulder clasp from the Sutton Hoo ship-burial 1, England. British Museum. CC BY-SA (https://creativecommons.org/licenses/by-sa/2.5)

Library of Congress Cataloging-in-Publication Data

Names: Veach, Dan, 1948- translator.
Title: Beowulf & beyond : classic Anglo-Saxon poems, stories, sayings, spells, and riddles / Dan Veach.
Other titles: Beowulf and beyond | Beowulf. English.
Identifiers: LCCN 2020047107 (print) | LCCN 2020047108 (ebook) | ISBN 9781948488617 (paperback) | ISBN 9781948488624 (pdf)
Subjects: LCSH: English literature—Old English, ca. 450-1100—Modernized versions. | Anglo-Saxons—Literary collections.
Classification: LCC PR1508 .B46 2021 (print) | LCC PR1508 (ebook) | DDC 829/.08—dc23
LC record available at https://lccn.loc.gov/2020047107
LC ebook record available at https://lccn.loc.gov/2020047108

Printed in the United States of America on acid-free paper.

Beowulf & Beyond

*Classic Anglo-Saxon Poems,
Stories, Sayings, Spells, and Riddles*

Dan Veach

LOCKWOOD PRESS
Atlanta, GA

Contents

Foreword

What a golden hoard of Anglo-Saxon Dan Veach has delved up for us: prose, riddles, spells, *Beowulf* and more, polishing away the grime of centuries so they shine as though freshly fashioned. I cannot think of a more deeply learned translator who, at the same time, wears his learning so lightly, locating each work with a brief introduction and letting its humanity gleam through. I was especially intrigued to see how he brings women to the fore here, as warriors, peace-weavers, and speakers with their own voices. The modern language is clear and uncluttered, with just enough color, melody, and flavor of old English ("dawn-sorrow"; "summerlong"; "mind full of murder") to delight the eye, ear, and palate.

— A. E. Stallings

Preface

This book allows us, like Bede's sparrow, to fly into the fire-lit hall of Anglo-Saxon culture and enjoy the astounding feast set out before us. All the best stories are here, the most magical spells, the most ribald riddles, the most inspired flights of song.

The main course, of course, is *Beowulf*, a great wild boar of a poem whose flavor is like nothing else on earth. As the golden cup is passed around, we sit as close as we can to the music of the ancient poet's harp, the mead-sweet honey of his song.

There's plenty of good English beef here too, some of it bloody. "The Battle of Maldon," one of the world's great war poems, puts us on the front line against the Viking onslaught, surrounded by shouting men, clanging swords and whistling arrows. Women also win their share of honor: Judith is as handy with a sword as Beowulf—maybe more so, as he keeps breaking his!

Their brand of Christianity was no place for cowards either. In "The Dream of the Rood," Christ is a courageous young warrior, eager for his encounter with the cross. They even dared to rewrite Genesis—and make the story better. In their version of *Paradise Lost*, Eve is innocent of any intentional sin. And Satan has a juicy new role—eight hundred years before Milton—as a dark, dramatic antihero, speaking from the depths of his rage and pride.

There is wine for the spirit as well: the vast elegiac vision of "The Wanderer" and the flight of the soul at the end of "The Seafarer," one of the great moments in all of world poetry. This new translation of "The Seafarer" was recently awarded the Willis Barnstone Translation Prize.

For dessert we'll unbutton a bit, and serve up some tidbits you won't find in the textbooks. There are curious sayings and spells, where Christianity and paganism intertwine. And we'll share in a favorite Anglo-Saxon pastime—telling riddles. Let the reader beware: "riddled" with innuendo, some of them would make Freud swallow his cigar!

It's amazing to us that such *risqué* riddles were found in a manuscript written by monks and owned by a bishop. But this is just one more example of the robust, broad-minded, warmly human worldview reflected in *Beowulf* and the other fare set forth here. It's a world we have much to learn from. Enjoy the feast!

Tales from the Venerable Bede

The Story of Caedmon

Caedmon, sing for me.

This story is recounted by the Venerable Bede (AD 632–735), the great historian of Anglo-Saxon England. It took place in the seventh century at the monastery of Whitby in England. This monastery was founded by a remarkable woman, Saint Hilda, who became its first abbess and a counselor of kings.

Caedmon was a humble cowherd at a monastery. He had never learned how to sing. And so, when the harp was being passed around at a beer party, and his turn was approaching, Caedmon quietly slipped away, going back to sleep in the stable. In a dream that night, a man greeted him by name, saying "Caedmon, sing for me."

Caedmon replied "I don't know how to sing—that's why I had to leave the party."

"But you *can* sing," the man said.

"What shall I sing?" Caedmon asked.

"Sing to me of the Creation."

Immediately, Caedmon began to sing:

Now let us praise the Ruler of heaven's realm,
the Creator's power and his wisdom,
the work of the glorious Father. For He,
the eternal Lord, in the beginning
established each and every wonder.
The holy Maker first shaped heaven's roof
for the children of men. Then God Almighty,
the eternal Master, Guardian of humanity,
made for mankind this middle earth.

"Caedmon's Hymn" is the first recorded Anglo-Saxon poem, and the first to translate Christianity into German heroic verse. Lest there be any doubt about the source of his inspiration, *eight* different names of God are included in these brief nine lines. "Middle earth" (*middanyeard*), made popular by J.R.R. Tolkien's *Lord of the Rings*, was in fact a common Anglo-Saxon term for this world, perched, in both Christian and pagan theology, between the gods above and the demons below.

Caedmon remembered his song the next morning, and it was greeted as a gift from God by Hilda, the abbess of the monastery. Caedmon became a monk, and spent the rest of his days turning stories from the Bible into English poetry.

Pope Gregory Sees an Angle

No, this is not a misprint, but a famous Papal pun. And a prophetic one too, for Pope Gregory (AD 540–604) was determined to make his pun come true. This story comes from Bede's *Ecclesiastical History of the English People*. After the encounter described here, Pope Gregory sent missionaries to convert the Angles and the Saxons to Christianity.

Holy Pope Gregory is truly the Apostle of the English nation, for through his counsel and mission he delivered us from devil-worship and converted us to God's faith....

It happened once, as it often does, that some English merchants brought their wares to Rome, and Gregory passed by the street where they were on display. He saw among the men some slaves. Their bodies were white, their features fine, their hair fair.

Gregory beheld those beautiful youths, and asked what country they came from. He was told they were from Britain, where everyone looked like this. Then Gregory asked if that country's folk were Christian or heathen. They told him they were heathen. Gregory gave a heartfelt sigh and said "Alas that men of such fair hue should be subject to the dark Devil!"

He asked what race of men they were. "Angles," they said. He replied, "Rightly are they called *Angles*, for they have an *angel*'s beauty. They would make fitting companions for the angels in heaven."

Story of the Sparrow

flitting swiftly, in through one window and out the other

In his *Ecclesiastical History of the English People*, Bede recounts the dramatic conversion of the Anglo-Saxon king Edwin to Christianity. While Edwin was considering conversion, a rival king sent an assassin to attack him with a poisoned dagger. Afterwards, Edwin vowed to convert—if the God of the Christians would help him get revenge. No doubt the missionaries explained that this was not quite in the spirit of the thing. Nevertheless, he soon won victory over his rival. Still not convinced, he called his counselors together to discuss the matter. One offered this sage advice:

(The translated passage below, and the poetic "translation" that follows, are by the renowned poet and classical translator A. E. Stallings.)

"Oh king, man's life on earth—to make a comparison for our uncertain span— seems to me like this: You are feasting with your thanes and your companions in the winter. The hall is warmed by a fire on the hearth, while outside storms of winter rain and snow rage everywhere. Then a sparrow comes flitting swiftly, in through one window and out the other. While inside, it is untouched by the storm, enjoying a brief space of summer skies. But soon, returning from winter into winter, it slips from your sight. Thus, man's life appears for a just little while. But of what follows, or what came before, we are utterly ignorant. So, if this new religion offers us more certainty, then we should follow it."

From the Venerable Bede

by A. E. Stallings

*…adveniensque unus passerum domum citissime
pervolaverit qui cum per unum ostium ingrediens,
mox per aliud exierit…*

Like the flight of a sparrow
Come in from a squall
Through a hearth-lit hall,
Fleeting and narrow,
Our time's but a splinter—
Nobody knows
Where it comes from, or goes,
But outside it is winter.
At the feast, the hounds bark,
The wine flows, the fires roar,
But the wind's at the door
And outside it is dark.

Bede's Death Song

Bede's disciple Cuthbert, in his letter on the death of his master, says that Bede was "well-versed in our songs" (*doctus in nostris carminibus*). He includes as an example this poem in Anglo-Saxon, which has come to be known as "Bede's Death Song."

Perhaps it could be compared to the death poems of the Zen masters. For a man who has devoted his entire life to God, it shows remarkable humility of spirit. And it reminds us of a passage in "The Seafarer" where "There is no man on earth so proud in spirit… / that he has no fear, at his setting forth to sea / about what his God will bring him."

About that necessary journey
no one is wiser than he needs to be
when he considers, before his going hence
how his spirit will be judged
for good or evil, after his day of death.

Blood & Battle

Viking Attack on Lindisfarne

Anglo-Saxon Chronicle

Lindisfarne was a Celtic Christian monastery on an island off the northeast coast of England. It is famous for its beautifully illuminated Lindisfarne Gospels, comparable to the Irish Book of Kells. This is the first recorded Viking attack in English history. Unfortunately it was not to be the last.

Anno dccxciii (AD 793)

Dire portents were seen over the Northumbrian land, frightening the people terribly. There were huge flashes of lightning, and flaming dragons were seen flying through the sky. Those signs were followed by a great famine. And a little after that in the same year, on the sixth of the Ides of June, a raid by heathen men destroyed, with looting and manslaughter, God's church upon the isle of Lindisfarne.

The Battle of Brunanburg

Anglo-Saxon Chronicle

This poem celebrates a victory by the Anglo-Saxons over the Vikings and Scots in AD 937. Olaf was the Viking king of Dublin; Constantinus was king of Scotland. Such was the battle's importance that it became known simply as *bellum magnum,* "the great battle." The descriptions of the enemy dead are especially touching.

King Athelstan, lord of men and giver of rings
with his brother, prince Edmund, everlasting fame
hacked out in battle with the broadsword's edge
at Brunanburg. They split the shield-wall,
these sons of Edward, hewed the tough linden wood
with their hammered swords. Sprung from a noble line
these brothers in the field against all foes
had always defended their land
their hoard and home.

       The enemy crumpled,
Scotsmen and ship-men, the Vikings
fell doomed. The field darkened
with the blood of men, from sun-up,
morning tide, when the greatest of stars
glides over the earth, God's bright candle,
until at last it settled and sank to rest.
There lay many a man drained by the spear,
men of the North struck down on their shields.
Many a Scotsman beside them,
weary, tired of war.

      West Saxon troops
followed the tracks of the enemy all day long
hewed down from behind those fleeing the battle
with swords grindstone-sharp. They never held back,
those Mercians, from hard hand-play with any man

who had crossed the rough ocean with Olaf
seeking land upon the sea's bosom, fated to fall
in the battle.

       Five young kings
lay on that field, put to sleep by the sword.
Likewise seven of Olaf's earls, and uncounted
ship-men and Scots. Fled from the scene
was the chief of those Northmen, driven back
to his ship's prow with his little troop.
Crowding onto the boat, the king pushed off
onto the yellow-brown waters,
saving his own life at least.

So also, amid the retreat, the crafty Constantinus
fled to his northern home. That hoary warrior
had no cause to boast of this sharing of swords.
His kinsmen had been hacked away,
friends fallen from him on the field—
that battle hit him hard. His own son he left
at the place of slaughter, a young man in the combat,
ground up with wounds. That grizzled old man
had no cause for bragging, mind full of malice,
about the clash of blades.

       Nor had Olaf more reason
to think the tattered remnant of his troops
had won the field, the crash of battle standards,
mingling of weapons, meeting of spears and men
on that slaughter ground—the game
they had dared to play with Edward.

The Northmen fled in their nailed ships—
as many as the bloody spear had spared—
to seek out Dublin, over the Sea of Storm's
deep waters, returning to Ireland ashamed.

So also the brothers, both together,
king and prince, returned to their homes
in the West Saxon land, exulting in victory.

They left behind them, feasting on corpses
the dark-coated one, the black raven
with its beak of horn. And the dun-coated one,
the eagle with its white tail, greedy war-hawk
enjoying the carrion. And that gray beast,
the wolf of the woods.

The books and the old wise men tell us
there was never such a slaughter on this island
such a feast for the edge of the sword
since the Angles and the Saxons
brave war-smiths, glorious nobles
sought out Britain
over the broad-brimmed ocean,
overcame the Welsh and won the land.

The Battle of Maldon

This battle took place in AD 991, in the reign of Aethelred the Unready. (His nickname Unraed means "ill-advised" or "foolish," not "unprepared.") A Viking fleet under Unlaf, which had been raiding the English coast, was met by aldorman Bryhtnoth and his Anglo-Saxons at Maldon.

The Vikings landed on an island, connected by a narrow land bridge to the shore. They were unable to cross as long as the English held the bridge. Eager for battle, Bryhtnoth pulls back and lets the Vikings wade across to land. Will this turn out to be *ofermod*, overconfidence leading to rash and *unraed* action?

The battle speeches in this poem contain the quintessence of the warriors' code of honor. Byrhtwolde's Great Exhortation, spoken as they prepare for their last stand, is one of the high points of Anglo-Saxon poetry.

(The first and last pages of the manuscript are missing.)

Byrhtnoth, the Saxon earl, responds to the Viking invasion

> … were broken.
> He ordered the men to abandon their horses,
> drive them away and set forth on the march,
> their minds firmly fixed on the handwork ahead.
> The kinsmen of Offa soon found
> that this earl would suffer no slacking.
> He let go his own beloved hawk
> to fly to the woods when he went forth to battle—
> by this men might know this nobleman
> would never weaken in the war
> once he laid hands on his weapons.

Likewise Eadric intended to support his prince,
his lord in the struggle, and went forth bearing
his spear into battle. He held to this thought—
as long as he could hold a shield and broadsword
he would stand by his oath
to fight before his lord in battle.

Then Byrhtnoth began to marshal his troops,
riding about, bidding them to stand
and hold their ground, to hold their shields
upright and firm in hand, and never fear.
Once he had that host in fighting trim
he dismounted from his horse among that folk
where he most loved to be—amid his hearth troops
whom he knew most loyal.

The Viking envoy speaks

Standing on the other shore, the Viking messenger
sternly called out, announcing in a threatening voice
to that man standing on the bank,
the message from the fleet:

"They have sent me to you,
those bold seamen,
and ordered me to tell you
that you must send them quickly
gold rings in exchange for safety—
it will be better for you to buy off
this spear-rush with your treasure
than for us to be dealing out hard battle.

"No need for us to destroy each other—
if you have riches enough, we are willing
to seal this peace with gold. If you,
the richest man here, should decide
to pay the ransom for your people, give
the seamen, according to their judgment,
treasure for truce, securing our protection.
We will take your tribute to our ships,
take to sea and leave you here in peace."

Byrhtnoth replies to the Vikings

Byrhtnoth held his shield aloft and spoke,
shaking his spear's slender ashwood shaft,
angry, without taking counsel
he gave answer:

"Do you hear, seafarers,
what this folk has to say?
The only tribute you'll get from us
is spears—
poisoned points and ancient swords.
The war-gear we intend to give
won't help you much in this battle.

"Seaman's messenger, go back and give
your folk a far less pleasant answer—
that here we stand, still in possession
of our honor, an earl and his troops
who fully intend to defend their homeland,
King Aethelred's earth, my own lord's
land and people. It's you heathens
who will fall in battle!

"Too shameful, it seems to me,
that you should take our treasure to your ships
without a fight, now that you have invaded
our country. No, you won't earn
our riches with so little work. Spear point
and sword's edge shall decide
the terms between us—grim war-play
before we ever give you tribute."

The armies confront one another over a river crossing.

Then he ordered his men to bear their shields
and stand together on the eastern bank.
There, for the water, neither host
could reach the other: a flood tide came in
after ebb tide, locking up the way.
Too long, it seemed to Byrhtnoth,
before they could bear spears together.
The River Pan now stood between the sides
arrayed for battle—the East Saxon front line
and the Vikings. Neither one could harm the other
except for those death carried off
through the arrow's flight.

       The tide went out.
The seamen stood ready, a host of Vikings eager
for war. But the hero who held the crossing—
his name was Wulfstan, Ceolan's son,
valiant among his kin—ran the first Viking
through with his spear. There stood with Wulfstan
two fearless men, Maccus and Aelfere,
a courageous pair with no intention
of fleeing from the ford. No,
they would stand staunch against the enemy
as long as they could wield their weapons.

All too clearly the Vikings could see
these bridge-guards were bitter fighters.
Better use guile, thought those hateful guests:
they begged to be allowed safe passageway
to bring their foot-soldiers over the ford.

Byrhtnoth, eager for battle, lets the Vikings cross.

Then the earl, in his overconfidence
gave up too much land to that hateful host.
Across the cold waters he called out
and all the men listened to Byrhtelm's son:

"Now we have cleared the way for you.
Come over quickly and join the battle.
God alone knows which of us
will rule this place of slaughter."

The murderous wolves then waded—
they were not afraid of a little water,
that Viking host, westward over the Pan.
Bearing their shields of linden wood across
the shining stream, the seamen came to land.
Against them, fierce and ready, stood Byrhtnoth
and his men. He ordered them to raise the shield wall,
to hold fast against the enemy. Now the fight
drew nearer—glory and battle. The time had come
when doomed men had to fall. Cries
and clamor arose now. The ravens
gathered, eagles eager for carrion.
There was uproar on earth.

Now hands let go of spears—
hard and file-sharp they flew.
Bows were kept busy, shields
seized the sharpened points.
The battle-rush was bitter: men falling
on every hand, young warriors dying.
Wulfmaer was wounded, Byrhtnoth's kinsman,
chosen by the clash of arms, his own nephew
fiercely hewn down by the sword.

They paid the Vikings back in kind:
I heard that Eadweard struck one
with his sword, not holding back
on his blow; the fated warrior falling
at his feet. His lord thanked him later,
his own thane, the first chance he got.

So they stood firm and resolute, those men
on the front line of battle, each eagerly intent
on who would be first to win the life
of a doomed man with his weapons.
The slaughtered fell to earth—the rest
stood steadfast. Byrhtnoth exhorted them,
urging each man to fight hard
to bring doom down upon the Danes.

The Vikings attack Byrhtnoth

Weapon raised under the shelter of his shield
a battle-hardened warrior charged them.
The earl rashly ran at him, each
intending evil to the other. The seaman
launched a spear made in the south
and wounded the people's lord.
With a thrust of his shield, the earl burst
the spear shaft—the spear point quivered
and sprang back out again. Enraged now,
he stabbed the bold Viking
who had wounded him. Wise in war,
the earl thrust his spear shaft
through the man's neck, his hand
seeking out his sudden attacker's soul.

Then he quickly speared another,
bursting his armor, wounding him in the chest
right through the ring mail—at his heart
stood a poisoned point.

The earl was glad—the brave man laughed
and gave his Creator thanks
for this day's work that God had given him.

Then a Viking warrior let go a spear.
It flew from his hand and pierced
Byrhtnoth's body through,
that noble thane of Aethelred.
Standing by his side was an ungrown youth,
a boy in the battle, who bravely
drew from his body that bloody shaft.

Wulfstan's child, the young Wulfmaer,
pulled the hard thing back out. The spear point,
which wounded his lord so grievously,
stayed stuck in the ground.

Now an armed warrior rushed at the earl
to rob and plunder him—his rings,
his chain mail and his jeweled sword.
From its sheath, Byrhtnoth drew
the broad and bright-edged sword
and struck him a blow on his armor.
Too swiftly, one of the seamen stopped him,
crippling his arm.

      His gold-hilted sword
fell to earth. No longer could he hold
that blade or wield his weapon.
Then that old soldier shouted out,
encouraging his men, urging them onward,
his good companions. But he could not
stand fast on foot for long.
He looked to Heaven:

      "I thank you,
Lord of Hosts, for all the happiness
I knew in this world. Now I have need
that you grant my spirit grace,
that my soul might on its journey
to your kingdom, Lord of angels,
go in peace. And I beg of you,
don't let these hell-fiends
abuse my body."

Then they hewed him down,
those heathen warriors,
and both men who stood beside him—
Aelfnoth and Wulfmaer too
lay next to their lord
when they gave up their lives.

Godric and his brothers flee

Then they turned tail and ran from the battle,
those who had no desire to be there:
Godric son of Odda was the first
to flee from the fight, leave behind
that good man who so often gave
him horses. He leaped into the saddle
of his own lord's horse, which was not right—
he and his brothers with him, Godwine
and Godwig galloped away, never caring
what would become of the battle, left
the war and sought the woods, fled
into its fastnesses and saved their skins.

And many more fled than was fitting
if they had only recalled all the favors
their lord had done them—just as Offa
on that very day had told him
at a meeting in the mead hall—
that many a man who spoke out bravely there
would not stand with him in his time of need.

The hearth-troops remain

So the people's prince was fallen,
Aethelred's earl. They could all see,
his hearth-troops, that their lord lay dead.
Still they stepped forth, those brave thanes,
undaunted men advancing eagerly,
all resolved upon one of two things—
to give up their lives, or avenge their lord.

Aelfwine's challenge

Aelfric's son encouraged them—
Aelfwine, young in winters, timely words
spoke out courageously—
                              "Remember now
the vows we spoke so often, sitting at our mead,
the boasts we raised from the benches—
heroes in the hall—about hard fighting.
Now we shall see how keen you are!

"I will make my lineage known
to all: I come of a noble family in Mercia.
Ealhelm was my grandfather's name,
wise alderman, blessed with this world's goods.
Let none of my people reproach me
that I would abandon this army,
run home now that my leader lies
hewn down in battle. My hurt
is the greatest here—he was both
my kinsman and my lord."

He stepped forth to settle that feud,
pierce one of the sea-folk with his spear point,
leave him laid out on the ground.
He urged his friends and companions
to follow him.

Offa's curse

Offa shouted, shaking his ashwood spear,
"Aelfwine, you have urged us all
to do what must be done.
Now that our lord lies dead,
the earl upon the earth, we must each
encourage the other to fight
for as long as we have and hold
our weapons—hard blades, spears
and good swords. Godric, Odda's son
has betrayed us all. Too many men
went with him when he took to horse,
exulting upon our lord's own steed.
So here on the field our folk was divided,
the shield wall broken. Damn his deed,
that put so many of our men to flight!"

Leofsunu's vow

Leofsunu spoke, his sheltering linden-wood
shield aloft, he addressed the men—
"I vow to you, from now until the end
I will not retreat a single step
but go forward to win revenge
for my lord and friend.
Nor need any steadfast Sturmere man
reproach me, now that my friend has fallen,
that I, lord-less, ran away home
from the war—no, I will hold firm
my weapons, spear point and iron."
Filled with wrath, he fought staunchly
with never a thought of flight.

Dunnere dares to speak

Dunnere then spoke up, a simple man,
he shook his spear and called out loud above them all,
bidding each man to avenge Byrhtnoth:

"Never flinch now if you mean
to revenge our master on these people—
and don't think twice about your life!"

Then they all charged forward, careless
for their lives, all the hearth-thanes
fighting hard. The grim spear-bearers
prayed to God they might avenge
their dear friend and bring destruction
on the enemy.

Even a Saxon hostage joins the fight

            One of the hostages
was also eager to wreak havoc—
he was of tough Northumbrian stock:
Ecglaf's son, his name was Aescferth.
Never one to run from war-play,
he kept up a rapid arrow fire—
sometimes they thumped on shields,

sometimes they tore through flesh.
Over and over he opened wounds
for as long as he could hold his bow.

Eadweard the Tall makes good his boast

Still in the line of battle stood
Eadweard the Tall, keen and eager
he spoke this boast: that not
one foot's length would he flee
back to where that better man lay.
He broke through the shield wall
and fought until his treasure-giver
was worthily revenged upon those seamen
before he too lay down amid the slaughter.

So did Aetheric, Sibyrht's brother,
that noble companion, eagerly press forward
fighting in deadly earnest, and many more like him,
cleaving the shield rims, warriors strong and keen.
Shields burst open, and the chain mail sang
a song of terror.

Offa fulfills his promise

      The seamen struck down
Offa in that battle, Gaddes' kinsman
fell to earth, sought out the ground.
He was swiftly hacked to death,
having done all his lord had asked of him.
He had vowed to his giver of rings
that they would both ride back to town,
come unharmed home, or fall together in the battle.
Wounded and dead on that slaughter-ground
he lay now, as a good thane should,
close by his lord.

The Viking charge

       Amid splintering shields
the Vikings charged in full battle rage,
spears punching clean through the husks
of doomed men's souls.

       Wistan then stepped up
to fight them, Thurstan's son. He was the third
to be killed in that rush; before him, Wigeline's son
lay down with the dead. It was a cruel meeting—
some standing their ground in the struggle,
others crumpling, weary of their wounds.
To earth fell the slaughtered.

All the while Oswold and Eadwold
the two brothers kept the troops in line
shouting encouragement to their comrades
that in this time of need they must bear up
and grasp their weapons firmly.

Byrhtwolde's Great Exhortation

Byrhtwolde now spoke out, raising
his shield aloft and shaking his spear.
An old retainer, he boldly addressed the troops—

Hearts must be keener, minds more determined,
spirits greater, as our strength grows smaller.

Here lies our lord cut down, the good man
on the ground. He will always regret it
who runs away now from this battle.

I am an old man. I will not leave this field.
Here, beside my lord, with these men I loved,
I intend to lie.

So too Aethelgar's son Godric
urged the men onward, throwing
the slaughter-spear over and over
at the Vikings, first in the charge
against that host, hewing about him

and laying them low, until he at last
fell in the fighting. This was not
the same Godric who fled from the battle....

Norman Invasion of 1066

Anglo-Saxon Chronicle

We come now to the climactic event of Anglo-Saxon history: the invasion by William of Normandy in 1066. Once more there were great portents seen in the sky—in fact, the "long-haired star" we now call Halley's comet. Things might have ended differently if the Anglo-Saxons had faced William alone. But they had *two* invasions to deal with. The English king Harold trounced a Norwegian force at Stamford Bridge, but then his exhausted army had to rush south to meet William at Hastings. There, after much hard fighting, Harold was killed (perhaps, as shown in the Bayeux tapestry, by an arrow in the eye) and the Normans won the day.

It was the end of the Anglo-Saxon era in England. History is notoriously written by conquerors, but here for once we have the other side of the story. The normally staid chronicler can hardly control his feelings as he records the Anglo-Saxon surrender. His anguished cry "that was the biggest mistake that men have ever made" is the same expression used to describe the Fall of Man in the Garden of Eden.

Millesimo lxvi [1066]

All over England there were signs in heaven such as no man had ever seen. Some say the star was a comet, which some call the long-haired star…..

Then came William earl of Normandy into Peavensey on the eve of St. Michael's mass [September 28]. And as soon as he crossed, he built a fort at Hastings. King Harold was informed of this and gathered a great army, which assembled at an old apple tree. And William suddenly came upon him unawares, before his folk could be put in order. But the king nevertheless fought hard against him, with those men who would follow, and there was a great slaughter on both sides.

There were slain Harold the king and earl Leofwine his brother and earl Gyrth his brother and many good men. And the French had possession of the place of slaughter, which God granted for the sins of the people….

Archbishop Aldred and the mayor of London wanted the young prince Edgar to be king, for which his birth well suited him. Eadwine and Morkere swore they would fight for him. But when promptness was needed, things were delayed, growing worse from day to day, as it turned out in the end.

William afterward went to Hastings, and bid any man come there who would bow to him. When he realized that no one would come to him, he raised his remaining army, and those since come to him over the sea, and raided all the land he came across until he came to Beorhhamstede.

Quickly archbishop Aldred and prince Edgar came to him there, and the earls Eadwine and Morkere, and all the best men of London, and bowed to him of necessity, after most of the damage was done—and that was the biggest mistake that men have ever made, one that God would not forgive, for our sins—and gave him hostages and swore him oaths. They swore they would hold him as their lord, though meanwhile he ravaged everywhere he went.

On Midwinter's Day archbishop Aldred sanctified him as king. And he promised and swore with his hand on Christ's book—before Aldred would put the crown on his head—that he would rule this nation as well as the best kings before him had done, if they would be loyal to him.

Nevertheless, he laid a terribly cruel tax upon the people. That spring he crossed the sea to Normandy and took with him archbishop Stigand, Aegelnath abbot of Glastonbury, prince Edgar, the earls Eadwine, Morkere and Waeltheof, and many other good men of England.…

He built castles far and wide across the country, cruelly oppressing the people, and ever since things have gotten much worse. May the end come when God wills it.

Love & Loss

The Seafarer

The wide sweep of this poem plunges into exile's icy depths, then soars to the heights of spiritual ecstasy. In between, we have deep insight into an Anglo-Saxon soul, torn between hobbit-like happiness at home and dangerous adventure on the high seas.

The text of the poem in the Exeter Book is problematic. This version omits a long sermon, tacked onto the end, which never refers to the poem. The cuckoo, out of place in the original, finds a perfect nest here. This translation was honored with the Willis Barnstone Translation Prize in 2011.

I can sing my own song true, and tell
of my journeys and trials, how I suffered
days of toil and hardship, heart's grief
endured in the ship's hold of sorrow,
the terrible rolling and plunging of the waves.

Harrowing night watch on the vessel's prow
was often my lot, as the boat beat and pitched
its way beneath the cliffs. My feet
felt the pinch of cold, chained
in fetters of frost. The clutch of fear
was hot around my heart; inward hunger
ate at my water-weary mind.

How little he knows
whose feet are planted safe
on solid ground, about this life of mine
on the ice-cold ocean, how winter-long
I walked the exile's tracks, hung with icicles,
bereft of friends. Showers of hailstones flew.
The only sound was the pounding
sea, the ice-heavy wave. Sometimes
the wild swan's song I took

for my pleasure, the gannet's cry,
the curlew's call instead of the laughter
of men, the seagull's mewing
instead of honey mead.

      Storms beat
against the stone cliffs, and the tern,
icy-feathered, cries out in reply. Often
the dew-feathered eagle screams.
No kinfolk to comfort and protect
the poor soul in need. The sad voice
of the cuckoo, watchman of summer, sings
foreboding sorrow, bitter in the breast.

He little knows, the much-blessed man,
what one endures who plants his footprints
on the paths of exile. He will hardly believe,
who owns this life's joys, proud and wine-happy,
safe and snug in the town, what I, worn-out, weary
must endure on the pathways of the sea.

Night shadows darken, snow comes
from the north. Hoarfrost binds
the ground; hail falls to earth,
the coldest of grains. And yet,
beating upon the heart, still it comes—
the urge to try
the play of the high sea's salt waves
for myself, the soul always spurring
the spirit to fare forth, and far hence
seek out foreign lands and people.

No man on earth is so proud in spirit
so great in his gifts, in youth so daring,
so bold in deeds, nor his lord so kind
that he has no fear at his setting forth to sea
about what his God will bring him.

But he pays no heed to the harp, nor to gifts of rings,
the joys of his wife nor this world's bliss
nor to anything else but the rolling of the waves.
He will always be restless who sets out on the water.

Trees take on flowers, turning towns fair,
meadows lovely. The whole world quickens—
all this recalls the eager spirit,
the soul to its journey, for one who intends
to fare far on the paths of ocean.

So now my heart soars up
out of its chest, and flies—
my soul across the seaways,
the kingdom of the whale, goes circling wide
over the surface of the world, coming back to me
eager and greedy. The lone flyer screams—
whetting the spirit irresistibly
over the whale-way, over the wide expanses of the sea.

The Wife's Lament

The wife's situation is a mystery. She has apparently been exiled by her husband, who is now in exile himself. Was she perhaps a "peace-weaver" like Hildeburh in *Beowulf*, caught in a violent feud that made her husband turn against her? His kinsmen are to blame, secretly plotting to send her away. Still, she has never stopped loving and longing for her man.

The ending, where her lord sits "under a stone cliff, frozen by storms" reminds us of "The Seafarer," whose speaker is also an exile. These two and the next poem, "The Husband's Message," are all found in the Exeter Book. Could their stories be related?

I utter this song, speak of my journey
in the fullness of sorrow. I can tell
what hardships I have suffered—
new or old, since ever I grew up,
they were never more than now.

My path of exile has always been repaid
with pain. Since first my lord parted
from his people, over the rolling waves
I have endured dawn-sorrow, wondering
where, in what land, he might be.

So I fared forth on this journey,
seeking to serve him,
a joyless exile in my bitter need.
His kinsmen secretly plotted
to part us as far as possible
in this worldly realm, living wretchedly,
leaving me in longing.

My master ordered me to take
this hard place as my dwelling.

No loved ones do I find here,
no loyal friends in this land,
and so my mind is mournful.

The well-matched mate I found
was a hard-luck man, melancholy,
concealing, beneath a blithe bearing,
a mind full of murder.

We often vowed that only death
and nothing else would part us.
All that is whirled away
as if our friendship never was.
Far and near I must endure
this hateful feuding with my best-beloved.

My man made me live in a forest grove
under an oak tree, in a cave.
Old is this hall of earth,
and I am full of longing!

The valley is dark, the mountain steep,
a bitter fortress overgrown with briars.
A place without joy.
Here I am cruelly oppressed
by my lord's leaving. My friends
are in the ground, the ones I loved
in this life now laid low.

Meanwhile, every dawn
I walk beneath this oak tree,
around this cave. There I must sit
the summerlong day. There I can weep
the many hardships of my exiled way.

And so I can never find rest
from my cares, nor all the longing
that this life begets in me.

She imagines her missing mate.

A young man will always have a troubled mind,
hard thoughts in his heart—

beneath his blithe bearing, a chest full of cares
and a throng of endless sorrows.

In his solitude he may be longing
for all his earthly joys—
he may be outlawed,
exiled far to foreign lands
where my lord sits, under a stone cliff
frozen by storms, the weary man,
his dreary hall flooded with water.

My friend suffers heartache, remembering
the place where he once knew joy.
Woe unto him who must live
his whole life in longing!

The Husband's Message

The poem is spoken by a "rune-staff," a wooden stick carved with runic letters—one way of conveying a secret message in those unlettered days. This poem and "The Wife's Lament" both mention the "vows spoken often" when husband and wife were still together. The two poems may well be a matched pair. If so, "The Husband's Message" brings a fitting conclusion to their trials and suffering.

The capital letters at the end stand for a runic code in the original, whose meaning we moderns, lettered or not, have yet to figure out.

Now, in secret, I will tell you
how I grew up, a child of the tribe of trees.
With me, men set out for foreign lands
over the salt streams. Often in boats
I sought where my lord might be
across the high seas.

Now I have come, on the deck of a ship.
Now you will know
what to think in your heart
of my lord's love.
I dare promise you will find it
to be gloriously true.

Listen! He who carved this wood
asks that you, arrayed in jewels, remember
the vows you spoke so often in the old days
when you lived in the mead-happy town,
sharing one country, able to enjoy your friendship.

A feud drove him forth from his people.
But now he bids me tell you joyfully
to stir the ocean's waters, once you hear
the cuckoo's mournful song upon the hill.

Do not let anything deter you
from that journey, nor any man alive
prevent that voyage. Seek out the sea,
the kingdom of the gull, and board a ship.
Sailing southward on the seaways
you will find a man there,
where your lord awaits you.

Nothing in this world would please his heart,
he told me, more than that almighty God
should grant the two of you to be together
ever after, giving jewel-studded rings
to warriors and companions.
He has enough finely-wrought gold
now that he rules a foreign kingdom,
noble warriors and a lovely land—
although my friend first went there
driven by necessity, shoving off his ship,
a young man on the waves and waterways,
eager to fare forth, rowing the ocean currents.

Now the man has overcome his hardship.
He would lack for nothing he desires—
neither horses nor treasure nor the joys of mead,
no wealth on earth, oh prince's daughter—
if he only had you, fulfilling that old vow
between the two of you.

I give you "S" and "R" together,
"EA," "W," and "M," and swear this oath—
that as long as he lives he will keep
the promise and the pledge of love
you made so often and so long ago.

The Wanderer

This vast and sweeping elegiac vision is one of the most beautiful Old English poems. The theme of the exile had great appeal to the Anglo-Saxons: in those days a man without a community's warmth and protection was truly miserable. We find surprising psychological depths here: the exile's dream and awakening are especially touching.

As in *Beowulf*, there is a mixture of pagan and Christian elements. The first verse evokes both the Christian God and the Germanic concept of *wyrd*, inexorable fate. And the hopeless pagan vision of a crumbling world leads naturally into Christian consolation at the end. Still, it is the bitterly cold, inconsolable pagan worldview which makes this poem so compelling.

Often a lonely man longs for mercy,
God's grace for him who, soul-weary,
over the waterways must row
the paths of exile, stirring the frost-cold sea.
There is no escaping fate.

So spoke the wanderer, calling to mind
cruel slaughter, the fall of friends.
At each day's dawn I must speak my sorrow
for there is no living creature now
I dare clearly tell my own heart's truth.

I know it is a noble virtue in a man
to bind fast the soul in his breast, guard
his heart's treasure, whatever he may feel.
The weary of spirit cannot withstand fate
nor can a troubled mind give any help.

Therefore those eager for glory
must lock thoughts of sorrow
in the heart's chest. And so must I,
often fearful, far from homeland

and the help of kinsmen, bound
in fetters since my gold-giving friend
was covered by the darkness of the earth.

I went from that place poor and winter-weary
homesick over the icy waves. I sought
far and near for a treasure-giver
in some mead hall who might know my people,
offer the friendless one some comfort,
give joy and delight.

He knows who has tried it, how hard it can be
to fare forth in sorrow, without a friend
to love and share his heart. For him
the tracks of exile, not the torcs of gold.
A heart of hoarfrost, not earth's happiness.
He remembers his hall mates, gifts of treasure,
how in his youth his gold-friend
used to feast him. A vanished joy….

So he will find, who has long been without
his friendly lord, beloved counselor,
when sorrow and sleep bind
that lonely man, he will dream
he clasps and kisses his lord again
and on his knee lays hand and head
as he used to do in bygone days,
in joy before the treasure-throne.

Then the friendless wretch wakes up,
sees before him brown waves,
seabirds bathing, spreading their feathers,
fierce frost and snow with hailstones mingled.

Now his wounded heart weighs heavier,
sore for his loved ones, sorrow
sprung afresh. As the man's mind and spirit
remember that joyful greeting,
he looks about him eagerly—
but his hall companions drift away,
their floating spirits bring him

few words of comfort. Care comes again
to him who must so often send
over the frozen waves his weary soul.

And so I cannot imagine why
my mood should not grow dark
considering this world and the life of men—
how suddenly proud warriors
must give up the hall, for every day
this middle earth is crumbling and falling.

No man can be considered wise
until he has his share of winters
in this world. A man must be patient,
never hot-headed nor too quick to speak.
In war, neither reckless nor weak,
not giving way to fear nor to elation.

Be not greedy for treasure. Nor should a man
be eager to boast before he knows for sure.
A bold spirit must hold himself back
before he speaks vows,
to see where his heart thoughts
will take him.

The wise man knows how ghastly it is
when all this world's wealth
lies in waste—just as now, scattered
about this middle earth, stand walls
crusted with frost, storm-beaten,
crumbling halls of happiness
whose lords lie now bereft of pleasure.
Their noble troops all fallen
proud before their walls, seized by war
and carried off to the hereafter—
some borne by birds of prey
over the high seas; some by the hoary wolf
dealt death; some buried by men,
tearful and grave, in caves of earth.

This place so ravaged
by mankind's Creator,
bereft of the sounds of its citizens,
this ancient work of giants
now stands empty, desolate.

He who upon these ruined walls
has well and truly thought, and this dark life
deeply pondered, wise in spirit,
remembers far off, again and again
so many slaughters, and speaks these words:

Where is the horse? Where is the man?
Where is the treasure-giver?
Where are the joys of the hall?

Alas for the shining cup!
Alas for the chain-mailed warrior!
Alas for the people's pride!

How time has passed away
grown dark beneath the helm of night
as if it had never been!

There stands now, all that's left
of that beloved company,
a wall wondrous high, writhing
with the shapes of worms.

Men carried off by a multitude
of spears—weapons greedy for slaughter—
that glorious fate.

            And now on this rocky cliff
storms beat and snowfall binds the earth,
the onslaught of winter. Then comes the dark.
Night shadows deepen. From the north
a hailstorm lashes out, full of malice for men.

All is hardship upon earth's kingdom.
Fate follows its course throughout creation,
this world under heaven:

Here wealth is fleeting.
Here friends are fleeting.
Here man is fleeting.
Here family is fleeting.

The framework and foundation of this world
Is all in vain!

So the wise man said in his heart,
sitting apart in meditation. Worthy is he
who guards his good word, never speaking
the passions in his breast too recklessly—
until, with his courage, he can find
a remedy.
   All will be well
with him who seeks for mercy, comfort
from the Father in Heaven. There, for us all
stands our security.

Bold Spirits

Satan's Rebellion

From the Anglo-Saxon Genesis

With bold imagination, the poet turns Satan into a dark, dramatic antihero, hundreds of years before Milton's *Paradise Lost*. It is at least possible that Milton heard of this version—he was friends with the scholar Junius, who owned the manuscript.

The language of the Anglo-Saxon Genesis indicates that it came from two different sources: an early manuscript (Genesis A), and a later account of Satan's rebellion and the Temptation (Genesis B), from which the next two excerpts are taken. Genesis B seems to have been translated from an Old Saxon original. The Anglo-Saxons were very interested in bringing Christianity to Anglia and Saxony, their old homelands in Europe, and the effort was evidently paying off.

God creates Lucifer

One He had worked with such strength,
so mighty in his mind and thought,
that He granted him the greatest power,
highest next to Him in Heaven's kingdom.
He had made him so radiant,
so fair his form among the hosts of Heaven
that he blazed like a brilliant star....

Dear as he was to our Lord,
it could not be kept secret from Him
that his angel was growing arrogant.
He raised himself up against his Master,
spoke hateful, boasting words, refusing
to serve God, declaring that his own body
was lovely and light-filled,
glistening, shimmering.

He could not find it in his heart
to give the Lord his loyalty and service.
He thought he had more strength and skill,
more angel hosts to follow him
than holy God himself.…

"Why should I slave?" said he.
"I have no need for a master.
With my own hand I can work so many wonders.
I have the power to raise a greater throne,
higher still in Heaven. Why should I be subject
to His pleasure, bow to Him in servitude?
I can be God as well as He!"

Then the Almighty was filled with wrath,
high Heaven's guardian, and threw him down
from his lofty throne.…
Three long days and nights
he and his angels fell from highest Heaven
into Hell, and God turned them all
into devils.…

There, through nights immeasurable
each fiend suffers everlasting fire.
Then at dawn comes an eastern wind,
frost wickedly cold. Forever fire
or spears, some terrible torment
they are doomed to suffer.

Satan plots vengeance on God and Man

"He has not done right
to fling us into the fire's depths
in this place called Hell,
depriving us of Heaven's kingdom—
which He now intends to settle
with Mankind.

"That burns me most of all,
that Adam—made of *dirt!*—
should sit upon my mighty throne,
filled with joy, while we must suffer
punishment and torture here in Hell.

"Oh, if my hands were freed
and I could fly from here just once,
for one short winter hour.
Then I and this mighty army....

"But no. I lie here in hard irons,
huge bars hot-forged and hammered.
God has chained me by the neck.
So I know that He has read my mind
and realized that evil would befall
between the two of us, myself and Adam,
disputing over Heaven's kingdom,
if only I had the free use of my hands!

Satan asks for a volunteer

"If I ever gave any thane princely treasures
in years gone by, when we dwelt in happiness
in that good kingdom, and held our thrones,
there would never be a better time
to repay my gifts than now.

"If any thane of mine were able
and willing, he might fly up
out of this prison on feathered wings,
winding his way among the clouds
to where Adam and Eve, new-created
live lapped in abundance
on their earthly realm—while we
are thrown in this deep abyss.

"Now *they* are more beloved by the Lord.
Now *they* possess the wealth that we
should rule by right in Heaven....
Think about this, every one of you—
think how we can betray them!
I would rest more softly in my chains
if they should lose their kingdom."

The Temptation

From the Anglo-Saxon Genesis

The Anglo-Saxons had a high regard for women, and it shows in this retelling of the Fall of Man. Rather than yielding to pride or greed as in the original, Eve is doing her best to serve God and save a "rebellious" Adam. Her only problem is that the angel she has trusted comes from Satan. But she is an innocent victim, blameless by any human standard.

One of Satan's angels escapes from Hell

Then God's enemy girded himself
eagerly in his armor. He had treachery in mind.
He put the helmet of invisibility
upon his head and buckled it tight.
He knew a lot of clever speech
and twisted words. Determined
and resolute, he made his way upwards,
escaping the gates of Hell....

He took on a serpent's form
and wound himself, with devil's craft,
about the Tree of Death. He plucked
the fruit growing there, then went to find
the handwork of Heaven's Creator.
The hateful thing began to question him
with lying words:

"Have you any longing, Adam,
to rise up to God?"
I was sent here from afar
upon an errand for Him—not long since
I was sitting by His side. He ordered me

to make this journey. And He orders you
to eat this fruit.

He says your strength and power
will increase, your soul grow larger,
your body will be filled with greater light....
Serve Him with gladness—take this fruit
in your hand, and take a bite.

Adam answers

"When I heard the victorious Lord,
the mighty God speak out
in a powerful voice, He ordered me
to dwell here and keep His commandments.
He gave me this lovely woman for my wife,
and warned me not to be deceived
by the Tree of Death....

"You are not like any of His angels
I have ever seen....
I can't listen to you. Go away!
I believe firmly in almighty God
who made me with His arms,
with His own hands. He can give me
any good from His high realm—
He has no need to send a messenger."

The angel replies

"I know our Lord God will be angry
when I fare far to bring Him
this message: that you refuse
to obey the commandment sent to you
on this journey from the East.
Now He will have to come Himself
to answer you, since His messenger
cannot deliver His command. And I know
He will be furious in His mighty heart
against the two of you....

He turns to Eve

"Consider in your breast
how you may turn His wrath away
from both of you, as I have shown you.
Eat of this fruit! Your eyes
will be filled with such light
that you can see through all the world,
even to your Lord's own throne,
and enjoy His favor ever after….

"If you fulfill this behest, oh best of women,
I will conceal from our Lord that Adam
spoke such harsh and hateful words to me—
accusing me of falsehoods, saying I was eager
to do him harm, a servant of the Devil,
not God's angel."

He led her on with lies
and alluring seductions, tempting
the woman to that sin, until
the serpent's thoughts welled up
within her (God had made her
the weaker spirit), and her heart
was inclined to his council.

From the enemy, against God's word
she took the bitter fruit
of the Tree of Death. Never
was a worse deed done by man!

Eve pleads with Adam

"Adam, my lord, this fruit is so sweet,
bringing joy to the heart,
and this beautiful messenger
is God's good angel. I can see
by his clothing that he is a servant
of our Master, Heaven's King.

"It will be far better for us
to win His favor than His wrath!

If you have spoken harmfully today,
He will still forgive us
if we will only do His will.

"Why strive so hatefully
against your Master's messenger?
We need his favor—
he can plead for us
before the Almighty, King of Heaven.

"I can see far off to the south and east
where He who made the world
sits wrapped in splendor. I see
His angels in their feathered robes
circling about Him, the greatest
and most beautiful of hosts.
How could such knowledge
be given me, if not by God?

"I can see far and wide across Creation.
I can hear the sounds of joy in Heaven.
My soul is radiant inside and out
since first I tasted of this fruit."

The most beautiful of women spoke to Adam
over and over, laid it on so thick
the thane began to waver in his thoughts,
believing what the woman bid him do.

She acted purely out of loyalty,
never suspecting that so many evils,
such dire afflictions would follow for mankind
when she took that hateful messenger's advice
to heart. She only hoped to win
God's favor with her words.

Adam eats the fruit

From the woman
he took Hell and death—
they were not called that,
but bore the name of "fruit"....

Once it had penetrated deep inside,
seizing hold of his heart,
the evil-minded demon laughed aloud,
dancing and clapping his hands,
giving thanks to his lord for the two of them ....

"May your heart be blithe and merry
in your breast! Two things have been done today.
The sons of men have lost their home in Heaven—
now they must come to you and burn in fire.
And we have hurt God Himself
and given Him heart-sorrow.

"Now my spirit has been healed,
my thoughts are once more light-hearted.
The injuries we suffered for so long
have been avenged. Now I will seek out Satan
and the fire, where he lies bound in chains
in blackest Hell."

The Sacrifice of Isaac

From the Anglo-Saxon Genesis

Bede tells us that Caedmon translated Genesis into verse. So it is possible that this story of Isaac, from the older Genesis A manuscript, may have been composed by Caedmon himself. The touching human drama of Abraham's sacrifice is brought out more effectively than in the biblical account. Though it probably never occurred to anyone, Abraham is rewarded for doing precisely what Eve was punished for: taking the word of an angel that God had changed His mind.

Then the mighty King began to try the man,
eager to see what kind of courage
that noble soul possessed. Aloud, He spoke
these stern, harsh words to him:

"Go quickly, Abraham—
make tracks, and take
your only son with you.
You shall sacrifice Isaac to me,
make a victim of your son,
after you climb the steep mountain,
with your own feet tread
the high ridge I shall show you.

"There you shall prepare a flaming pyre,
a balefire for your boy,
and you yourself shall sacrifice
your son with the sword's edge.
Then the dark flames
will devour that beloved life
and you will offer him to Me.

The noble man went with his own son
into the wilderness. God showing the way,
they walked through the forest.
The son carried the wood,
the father, fire and sword.

Then the boy, young in winters,
asked of Abraham:
"We have fire and sword here, dear father,
but where is the sacrifice
that you intend to give bright God
as a burnt offering?"

Abraham answered—
he had but one thought,
to do as God commanded him—
"The True King, Guardian of all mankind,
will find one for Himself
as He sees fitting."

Stern and determined, he climbed
the steep mountain with his offspring
as the Eternal had commanded,
until he stood upon the peak of that high place
where the firm words of the ever-faithful God
had guided him.

He began to build up the pyre
and kindle the flame. He bound
his son, young Isaac, hand and foot
and hefted him onto the funeral fire.

Quickly he grasped the sword by the hilt—
he was going to kill his only son
with his own hand, let the fire drink
the blood of his boy.

Then an angel from above,
one of the Creator's thanes,
shouted loudly: "Abraham!"

He stopped, stock still
when he heard that angel's cry.
Quickly, from on high in Heaven
God's glorious spirit spoke to him:

"Beloved Abraham, do not slay
your own son, but quickly take
your offspring off the fire—
God has granted him glory.

"Man of the Hebrews, you will be blessed
by the sacred hand of Heaven's King
with the true rewards of victory,
an everlasting gift. The Guardian of souls
grants you His favor
because His friendship and His grace
were more dear to you than your own child."

The Dream of the Rood

This poem delves into the central paradox of Christ's cross: a shameful punishment for criminals that became the glorious symbol of salvation. In keeping with German heroic tradition, Christ is presented as an eager young warrior, acting joyfully rather than suffering passively. This re-visioning of the central event of Christianity was even bolder than rewriting Genesis.

Lines from this poem were inscribed in stone on the Ruthwell Cross, circa AD 700.

Listen! I will tell you the choicest of dreams
which came to me at midnight
when all who bear human speech
were fast asleep.

I thought I saw the most marvelous tree,
the brightest of beams,
rising into the sky all wreathed in light.

That beacon was drenched in gold, and beautiful gems
were scattered over the surface of the earth. Likewise
five jewels were shining across the shoulder span.
All of God's angels, eternally lovely, beheld it there.

To be sure, this was no gallows
for a criminal—holy spirits gazed upon it
along with men across the earth
and all this great creation.

Wondrous was that triumphant tree,
and I all stained with sin, wounded by wickedness.
I saw its wood in glorious raiment, radiant with joy—
that tree of the forest arrayed in gold
and crusted with jewels splendidly.

But I could still see through the gold
the signs of a terrible, earlier agony.
As it began to bleed on the right hand side
sorrow stirred within me. I was in fear
at that fair sight. I saw that shining beacon
change clothing and color—
sometimes it was soaked and wet,
drenched with the flowing blood,
and sometimes adorned with treasure.

Still I lay there for a long time
sadly gazing at the Savior's cross
until at last I heard the best of trees
begin to speak:

"It was long ago—I remember it well—
that I was cut down at the forest's edge,
taken from my trunk. Strong foes seized me,
made me into a spectacle, ordered me
to lift their enemies up.
Men bore me on their shoulders
until they set me on a hill
where my foes fixed me in place.

"Then I saw the Lord of all mankind
hurrying, with great zeal and courage
to climb upon me. There and then
I did not dare to break or bend
against God's word, when I saw
the earth begin to tremble.
I could have struck down all those enemies,
but I stood fast.

"The young hero, who was God Almighty
strong and resolute, stripped off His clothes
and mounted the high gallows
bravely, for everyone to see,
intent on freeing all mankind.

"I trembled when the Son embraced me.
I did not dare to fail or fall to earth—
I must stand fast.
I was raised up as the Rood,
bearing the mighty King aloft,
the Lord of Heaven—I dared not bend.

"They drove the dark nails through me.
The wounds are plain to see—open, evil gashes.
But I dared not do harm to anyone.
They mocked us both together.
I was all covered and soaked
with blood from the side of the Man
after He sent forth His spirit.

"Many fierce and bitter blows of fate
I endured upon that hill.
I saw the Lord of Hosts
stretched out in grief.
Darkness had overcast the Savior's corpse.
Over that bright radiance a shadow crept,
black beneath the clouds.

"All creation wept,
mourning the fall of the King—
Christ was on the cross!

"Men hurried to the Prince from far away—
I saw all that. Sorely troubled
as I was with sorrow, still I bowed down
to their hands, humble and filled with zeal.
They took hold of Almighty God,
lifting Him up from His bitter torment.

"The warriors left me, wet with blood
and wounded all over with spikes.
They laid Him down, limb-weary,
and standing by His head
beheld the Lord of Heaven.
He rested there a little while,
worn out from His great struggle.

"They began to build Him a house of earth
within sight of his dying place,
carving it out of bright stone
they laid the Lord of victory there
and sang a song of sorrow,
grief-stricken in the eveningtide.
Exhausted, they left their glorious Lord.
He rested there with little company.

"After the warriors went away
we stood there, stock still, weeping.
The body, fair house of the soul,
grew cold. Then a man felled us all
to the ground, a fearful fate,
and buried us deep in a pit. But friends,
the Lord's thanes, found me there
and arrayed me in silver and gold.

"So now you can see, my beloved man,
how I endured the work
of those who dwell in evil,
painful sorrow. Now the time has come
that I am honored far and wide.
Men from across the earth
and all this glorious creation
now pray to this symbol and sign.

"God's Son suffered
upon me for a while.
So now I tower, glorious under Heaven.
I can heal anyone
who holds me in awe.

"I was once the most terrible torture,
most hateful to men, but then
I opened up the way of life
to all who bear voice or tongue.

"And so the King of Glory,
the Guardian of Heaven exalted me
over all the forest trees
just as almighty God exalted His mother,
Mary herself, before all men,
above all womankind.

"Now I ask you, my dearly beloved,
to tell of this vision, revealing in words
that this is the glorious wood
where God almighty suffered
for mankind's many sins
and Adam's ancient deeds.

"He tasted death there
but afterwards the Lord arose
through His great might, to help humanity.
He ascended to Heaven, but he will once again
make his way to this middle earth.
The Lord himself, almighty God
amid his angels on the Judgment Day
will seek out all mankind.

"Then He who wields justice and authority
will judge each and every one
according to what he has earned
in this fleeting life.

"Nor can anyone be free of fear
of the words his Ruler will speak.
He will ask the multitude: where is the man
who would taste bitter death
for his Lord's name, as He did on that beam?
Then they will cower afraid,
scarcely able to imagine
what answer they could give to Christ.

"But no one needs to be afraid
who holds within his heart the best of beacons.
Through the Rood shall they seek the kingdom:
every soul that, abandoning earthly paths,
wishes to dwell with its Creator."

Then I prayed to that beam
with a joyous heart and abounding zeal,
alone as I was, with little company.
My spirit was on fire to set forth
upon the path, and often filled with longing.

It is now my life's joy
to seek alone for that victorious tree,
to honor it more than all the rest.
The will to do this fills my heart
and I look for my protection to the Rood.

I have few friends with power here on earth:
they have gone forth from this world's joys
to seek out the wondrous King. They live now
in Heaven with the high Father, dwelling in glory.

And every day I look forward to the time
when the Lord's Rood, which I beheld
here on earth, will fetch me from this fleeting life
and bring me where bliss is abounding,
to the joys of Heaven. There God's folk
are seated at the feast. There is endless happiness.
And He will set me there, where ever after
I will dwell in glory, and partake
of the joys of the holy.

May the Lord be my friend,
who suffered here on earth
for the sins of men
upon the gallows tree.
He set us free and gave us life,
a home in heaven. Joy was renewed
with bliss and blessings
for those who had come through the fire.

The Son was victorious in that struggle,
returning, mighty and triumphant
with a great host of spirits, a multitude
to the realm of God, almighty Ruler,
to the great joy of the angels
and all the saints dwelling in glory,
when their Lord came back, almighty God,
to where His kingdom was.

Judith

The Anglo-Saxons found much to their liking in the Old Testament, stories of war and intrigue perfectly suited to the poetic tools at hand. A society that admired strong women, they were especially tickled to find a brave warrior in Judith. She is not exactly a Brunhilde, stronger than any man but Siegfried. Judith is a wise, modest, curly-haired maiden (think of Shirley Temple with a sword) who risks her life and honor for her people.

The big battle scene is duck soup for the poet, of course, and he throws in the kitchen sink, including the Anglo-Saxon "beasts of battle": the raven, the wolf, and the eagle. One of the most hilarious scenes in Anglo-Saxon poetry comes near the end, when the Assyrian officers gather around the tent of Holofernes, clearing their throats loudly, afraid to awaken their general, who is "dead asleep."

The first part of the manuscript is missing. The Assyrians, the most feared warriors of the ancient world, were ravaging Israel. Judith, playing a dangerous game, intends to seduce their leader, Holofernes.

... [Judith did not] doubt the gifts [of God]
in this wide world. In her time of greatest need
she found the glorious Lord prepared
a shelter for her, favor from the highest Judge.
The Ruler of creation would protect her
against the worst terror.
The glorious Father in Heaven granted this,
for her faith in the Almighty
was always firm.

I have heard that Holofernes
was eager to throw a wine party,
to serve up a wondrous, magnificent feast.
That master of men
ordered all his thanes to come.

In a great hurry the shield-warriors obeyed,
came running to their mighty lord, the people's chief.

This was the fourth day since Judith,
wise in thought and lovely as an elf,
had sought him out.

X

Proudly they sat down to feast
and drink wine, those bold, well-armed warriors,
his companions in crime. Deep bowl after bowl
was borne among the benches,
full cups and flagons for the seated guests.
Those famous fighting men
were doomed as they drank, although
their mighty and terrible leader did not know it.

Holofernes, gold-friend of his troops,
was roaring drunk, laughing and bellowing,
whooping and hollering, so the sons of men
could hear from miles away
how that hard-minded man stormed and yelled.
Proud and lusty in his cups,
he urged the bench-sitters over and over
to buck up and bear themselves well.

So that malicious man, tough treasure-giver
drenched his men all day in wine
until they lay in a stupor, as though struck dead,
all of his veteran troops completely soaked
and drained of any good.

Thus their chief filled up his guests
until night's darkness neared the sons of men.
Then that corrupt and evil man
ordered them to bring the blessed maid,
adorned with rings and decked in jewels,
to his bed without delay.

His attendants quickly did as their chief,
ruler of armored warriors, ordered.

With clang and din they advanced
to the chambers of the guests.
There they found Judith,
wise in spirit. The shield-warriors led
that radiant maiden to the high pavilion
where the ruler Holofernes, hateful to the Savior,
always slept.

There was a fly net, fair and golden,
hung about the ruler's bed
so that the baleful lord of warriors
might look through at any son of man
who came there. But none could look on him,
unless that bold man called some warrior,
strong in evil, close to him for counsel.

Quickly they put the wise woman
in his bed. Then the stout-hearted heroes
went to let their lord know they had brought
the saintly maiden to his tent. At that,
the famous chief grew joyful—
he intended to stain and defile
that radiant lady sinfully.

But the Judge of glory, the wondrous Shepherd
was not to allow it. The Lord and Creator of hosts
held him back from such things.

Diabolical, filled with lust,
he left his troops and sought his bed
with evil on his mind. There he let go
of his earthly glory suddenly, in a single night.
The end of his time on earth would not be soft,
but such as the hard-hearted lord
had earned and worked for while he walked
this world beneath the roof of heaven.

He fell into bed so drunk with wine
there was no sense left
in the coffers of his wit. His warriors,
wine-weary, left quickly.

They had led that oath-breaking, hateful tyrant
to bed for the very last time.

Now the Savior's handmaiden,
filled with glory, gave serious thought
to how she might best take the life
of that terrible man, before the foul thing,
filled with sin, could awaken.

The Creator's maiden with her curling locks
took hold of a sharp sword
hardened in the storm of battle
and drew it from its sheath with her right hand.
She called on Heaven's Guardian by name,
the Savior of all who dwell here on earth,
and spoke these words:

"God of creation and comforting Spirit,
Son of the Almighty, I ask your mercy
in my great need, oh glorious Trinity!
My heart is on fire now, my spirit
sorely troubled with sorrow. Grant me,
Lord of Heaven, true faith and victory
so that I might with this sword
cut down this lord who gives not rings
but murder.

"Give me success, strong-minded Lord of men.
I have never had greater need
of your grace. Deliver me
from this storm in my spirit,
this fire in my breast."

Then the highest Judge
instantly inspired her with courage,
as He does for anyone who seeks His help
with wisdom and true belief.
Her soul grew larger. Hope sprang anew
for the holy maiden.

She grabbed the heathen firmly by the hair
and pulled his head towards her,
putting him to shame.
Deftly, she placed her evil foe
where she could deal with the wretch most easily.

The curly-haired lady
struck a bitter blow at her enemy
with a bloodstained sword—
shearing halfway through his neck
as he lay there in a stupor,
drunk and sorely wounded.

He was not quite dead—
his soul had not departed yet.
A second time
the courageous lady struck with all her might
at that heathen hound, so that his head
went rolling on the floor.

The foul basket of his flesh
lay empty once his soul had fled
beneath that deep cliff, there to be abased,
condemned to torment for eternity,
wound about with snakes, bound tight to pain,
chained hard in hellfire after his journey hence.

Wrapped in darkness, he need never hope
to leave that hall of serpents.
Always and forever, without end
he must dwell in that house of darkness,
deprived of hope and joy.

XI

Judith had won great glory in battle
when God, the Lord of Heaven
granted her the victory.
Then the wise maiden
quickly put the warrior's bloody head
in the bag that her pale-cheeked servant,
a worthy woman, had brought their food in.

Judith handed the gory thing to her prudent maid
to carry home. Courageous and triumphant
the two brave women took their leave
traveling straight from the army's camp
until they could clearly see the shining walls
of the beautiful city of Bethulia.

Adorned with rings, they hurried along the path
until they gladly arrived at the gate
in the city's wall. Within the fortress
warriors waited, awake and keeping watch,
as Judith, that sharp-witted maiden
had bidden her grieving people do
when the daring lady set forth on her journey.

The beloved one had come back to her people.
The wise woman quickly commanded
that someone from that spacious town
come let her in through the wall gate
right away. She spoke these words
to those triumphant people:

"I can tell you thankful tidings
so you need mourn no longer.
The Creator, King of glory,
has been pleased with you,
proclaiming across the whole wide world
that a brilliant victory is coming
with great splendor—glory granted
in place of the hurt and harm you long endured."

The citizens were overjoyed
when they heard how that holy woman spoke
over the towering wall. The troops rejoiced,
folks hurried to the fortress gate,
men and women, old and young
in hosts and multitudes. Thousands came running,
thronging toward the maiden of the Lord.

Every heart in the mead-town was happy
when they heard that Judith had come back home.
Quickly, with reverence and humility
they led her in.

The wise woman, adorned in gold
ordered her prudent handmaid
to unwrap the warrior's head
and show it, bloody, to the city's people
as a sign of her success in battle.
The noble woman spoke to everyone:

"Here, victorious warriors, leaders of the people,
gaze openly upon the head
of that hated heathen warrior—
Holofernes, dead. The man
who committed the most crimes against us,
bitter sorrows. And would have added to his count
but the Lord would not grant him a longer span
to grieve us with his evil. With God's help
I took the life out of him.

"Now I urge every man,
every shield-warrior in the city
to be ready for battle
as soon as God the Creator,
the glorious King, sends his bright rays
from the east.

"Bring forth your shields
and armor to protect your chests.
Bear your bright helmets in among your foes
to cut down their leaders, war chiefs
fated to fall, with blood-stained swords

"Your enemies are doomed to death,
and you to win fame and glory
in the fight, as the mighty Lord
has shown you through my hand."

An eager troop was quickly equipped
and keen to take the field. Brave as kings,
the warriors and comrades went forth to the fight.
Bearing triumphant banners, heroes under helmets
set out from the holy city
at the day's first red light.

Shields clanged and resounded.
The lank wolf in the woods rejoiced,
as did the dark raven, a bird
eager for slaughter. Both knew
that the soldiers intended to give them
their fill of the doomed. On their tracks
flew the dewy-winged eagle, eager for prey.
With somber coat and horny beak, it sang
a song of war.

The warriors marched forward,
men bound for battle, covered
by curved wooden shields.
They had suffered abuse
from the foreigners, insults
from the heathens. In spear-play
they would pay the Assyrians back
for all those hardships as soon
as the Hebrews under their banners
came to the enemy camp.

Boldly they let fly showers of arrows,
battle-vipers firm and hard.
The raging warriors stormed and shouted,
sending their spears forth
into the hardened troop.
The natives of that land were up in arms,
advancing fiercely on the hated foe.

Brave and stout-hearted, they roughly awakened
their old enemies, weary with mead.
Hands brought forth from sheaths
swords shining and richly adorned,
with proven edges. They struck in earnest
at the evil Assyrian troops,
sparing no man alive in that army,
rich or poor, whom they could overcome.

XII

So the thanes pursued the foreigners
all morning long. The sentries could see
how fierce they were, how the Hebrews advanced
with powerful swings of their swords.
Sending word to their senior generals,
they fearfully wakened those mead-weary warriors
with tidings of the morning's terror,
the bitter play of weapons' edges.

Then, I hear, those men doomed to slaughter
instantly shook off sleep, and with weary hearts
thronged to the tent of the baleful Holofernes.
They meant to instantly inform their lord
about the battle, before the terror of the Hebrews
fell upon him.

They all believed that their lord
and the bright maid slept together
in the beautiful pavilion: the noble Judith
and that lecher, terrible and fierce.
There was not a single man
who dared to wake up that warrior,
to find out what he had done
with the holy maid, the lady of the Lord.

The force of the Hebrew folk came closer,
fighting stoutly with their hard war weapons—
the sword's hilt settling their ancient quarrel,
blood-stained blades repaying old grudges.
Assyria's glory was dimmed by that day's work,
its pride turned to shame.

Men stood about their leader's tent
sorely disturbed, their spirits darkened.
All together they began to cough,
to cry aloud and gnash their teeth—
deprived of God and goodness,
even their teeth came to grief.

As for their glory, that was at an end,
all of their success and deeds of valor.

What they wanted was to wake their lord,
but up to now they had no luck.
At last, one battle-hardened man was bold enough
to venture into that pavilion, driven by necessity.
He found, lying pale on the bed
his gold-giver, bereft of life,
his spirit fled. Cold with fear,
he fell to the earth at once, and in a fit
began to tear his hair and clothes.

He said to the dejected warriors
who stood outside:
"Here we can clearly see
our own approaching fate.
The terrible time is near
when we must perish,
lost, all of us together, in the battle.
Here, hewn by the sword,
lies our protector, beheaded.

With minds in turmoil
they threw their weapons down
and, sick in spirit, sought to flee.
Hot on their tracks, the mighty host fought on
until most of the army, felled in battle,
lay on the field of victory, cut down
by the sword, at the will of the wolves,
a comfort for the carrion-eager birds.

Those left alive of the hateful warriors
still fled, pursued by a Hebrew host
exalted in glory, granted victory by the Lord,
fair help from the Father almighty.

Boldly with their blood-stained swords
the valiant heroes cut a war path
clean through the enemy troop,
shearing through the shield wall,
hewing linden wood. The Hebrew host

was in full battle rage, eagerly craving
the conflict of spears.

On that ground, when heads were counted,
there fell the greatest part
of Assyria's nobility, that hateful kin.
Few returned alive to their native land.

The courageous men made their way back
amid the carnage, the reeking corpses.
There was time now for the native troops
to take from their enemy, despised and lifeless,
the gory spoils of battle: shining ornaments,
broad swords and shields, bright helmets,
precious treasures.

The guardians of their country
had gloriously overwhelmed the foe
upon that battlefield,
put their ancient enemy
to sleep with the sword.
They left them lying in a swath,
those men who, as long as they breathed,
had been the most hateful
of all living people to them.

For a month, the most famous of nations
with their curly hair, bold and exulting
carried to the shining city of Bethulia
helmets and daggers, gray armor,
battle-dress filigreed with gold,
more treasures than the wisest man could tell—
all won by the strength of the people
brave in battle beneath their banners
through the wise council of Judith
that courageous maiden.

As her own reward in that adventure,
the spear-brave warriors brought her
Holofernes' sword and bloody helmet
along with his broad armor
inlaid with red gold.

All the heirlooms and belongings
of that arrogant master of men
rings and glittering treasures they gave
to the bright, quick-witted lady.

For all this Judith gave the glory
to the Lord of hosts, who gave her honor
and renown in this worldly realm
as well as a heavenly reward,
victorious triumph on high
because she had true faith in the Almighty,
never doubting, in the end, of those rewards
she had yearned for so long.

For this let the dear Lord be praised forever
who, in His mercy, made the air and wind,
the sky and the spacious earth,
the raging oceans and the joys of Heaven.

Magic & Mystery

Magic Spells

These spells or charms are found in Anglo-Saxon medical manuscripts. The first is part of a ritual to cleanse and bless infertile land. It leaves "no stone unturned," appealing to both pagan and Christian deities for help. Tacitus in his *Germania* says that the ancient Angles were goddess worshippers, seeing the earth as their mother. "Erce" here may be identical to Nerthus, the Germanic earth goddess to whom human sacrifices were made in pre-Christian times.

To Heal the Land

(Metrical Charm 1)

Here is the cure to heal your land if it will not grow well, or if evil has been done to it through sorcery or witchcraft....

Erce, Erce, Erce, Mother Earth!
May the eternal Lord, the Almighty grant you
fields growing and thriving
fertile and strong
crops brighter, stalks taller
broad fields of barley
white fields of wheat
and all the soil's fruits.

May God and his saints in heaven grant
that His earth be protected
from fiends of every kind,
defended against every evil
sown by witchcraft across the land.
Now I pray to the Creator
who shaped this world
that never shall a cunning woman
nor a crafty man remove
these words we have spoken....

For a Swarm of Bees

(Metrical Charm 6)

Bees were highly valued in the days when honey was the only sweetener—and more importantly the source of honey mead! This charm is to keep a swarm of bees from flying off into the woods. Interestingly, it shows awareness that most bees are female.

For a swarm of bees, take some earth in your right hand, sprinkle it under your right foot, and say:

I hold it fast under my foot.
Listen! This earth has power
over every creature whatsoever,
over all spite and jealousy,
and all the tongues of men.

Then cast it over the ground where they are swarming, and say:

Settle down, triumphant women!
Settle down to earth!
Never fly wildly
away to the woods.
Be as mindful of my welfare
as a man is of his meat and land.

Charms for Childbirth

(Metrical Charm 8)

While some charms are simply "charming," these are a reminder of how hard it was for women in the days before modern medicine. Even conception was tinged with dread. But sound principles of psychology are evident in these rituals dealing with hope and fear and grief.

1. *At conception*

When a woman may be with child, she goes to bed with her husband and says:

Up I will get, over you I will step
with a live child, not with a dead one,
with a full-born, not with a doomed one.

2. *To nourish the unborn*

A woman who cannot bear a child takes a handful of milk from a cow of a single color. She sips it with her mouth, then goes to a brook and spews the milk into it. With the same hand, she takes a mouthful of the water and swallows it. She says these words:

Wherever I carry this wonderful child
It will grow strong from this wonderful food
I will have this child and go home

When she leaves the brook she does not look back or return. She goes into a different house than the one she came from, and there eats some food.

3. *When the child moves*

When a mother can feel that her child has quickened, she goes to the church, stands before the altar, and says:

Christ, I say to you, behold this child!

4. *For delayed birth*

A woman who cannot bear a child goes to a wise man's grave. She steps over the grave three times, and three times says these words:

This is to cure me of hateful late birth.
This is to cure me of dark black birth.
This is to cure me of hateful lame birth.

[A "black birth" was a dark-colored "blue" baby. A "lame birth" was an ineffectual labor.]

5. *For a stillborn child*

A woman who cannot give birth takes a clod from her own child's grave. She wraps it in black wool and sells it to the merchants, saying:

I have sold it, now you sell it
The black wool and its seed of sorrow

Maxims

Cotton manuscript, Maxims II

This odd poem, composed of sayings about the way things ought to be, reminds us of Browning's *Pippa Passes*, where

> *The lark's on the wing;*
> *The snail's on the thorn;*
> *God's in His Heaven—*
> *All's right with the world!*

The Anglo-Saxon God was in His Heaven, all right. But just as surely there were dragons in the caves and ogres like Grendel in the swamps and fens. And women, as always, worked their magic on men. The wedding "rings" referred to at the end were substantial bracelets and necklaces, feminine versions of the rings given to warriors, of which our tiny wedding rings are but a distant reminder.

"Is" (*biþ*) maxims:

A city is seen from far away,
wise work of giants when they walked the earth,
raising wondrous walls. Wind is swiftest in the sky.
Thunder is the loudest thing. Christ's glory is the greatest.

Fate is strongest, winter coldest.
Lent is greatest frost and longest chill.
Summer is sun-loveliest, when heaven's warmest.
Harvest is most glorious, when men gather up
the year's fruits God has given them.

Truth is clearest, gold and treasure dearest
to any man. Age is wisest,
for one who has endured much,
weathered many years ....

"Shall" (*sceal*) maxims:

A king shall rule the land.
A young prince shall encourage good companions
in battle and in giving rings.
A nobleman shall be brave.
A sword's edge shall endure
in war against a helmet.

The hawk on its glove
shall roam the wilds.
The wolf shall haunt the woods,
a solitary, wretched wanderer.
The boar, with its mighty tusks,
shall dwell in the forest.

Good deeds shall win glory in a kingdom.
A spear shall rest in the hand,
its shaft adorned with gold. Jewels
shall stand upon rings, high and proud.
A stream shall mingle with the sea waves.
A mast shall mount a ship to bear a sail.
A sword shall lie on the lap, a lordly iron.

A dragon shall dwell in a cave, old,
proud of treasure. The fish shall live in the water,
bringing forth its kind. A king shall reign in the hall,
giving out rings. A bear shall dwell in the wilderness,
old and terrible. Water shall flow,
flood-gray, from the hills. Troops shall gather
in glorious strength. A man shall be true
to his word, and wise.

The woods shall blossom, lovely upon the land.
The green mountain shall stand high
above the earth. God shall be in Heaven,
the Judge of deeds. A door shall stand in the hall,
the building's mouth. The boss shall stand
on the shield, firm fortress for fingers.
The bird on high shall row the air.

The salmon shall shoot quickly through the current.
Sky showers, wind-blown, shall fall on earth.
The thief shall set forth in dark and stormy weather.
The ogre shall dwell in the fens,
alone in the land. A maid shall seek a lover
with dark magic, if she does not succeed
in finding a man among her people
who will give her rings.

Riddles

from the Exeter Book

The Anglo-Saxons were fond of riddles, and theirs were delightfully vivid and lively. Some are so bawdy we can hardly believe they were found in the Bishop of Exeter's book. But aside from what some of them obviously *suggest*, all have another, more innocent answer. So even the monks could enjoy them—while teasing their blushing brothers about their "sinful" thoughts!

Riddle 25

I'm a wonderful creature,
a comfort to women
and useful to neighbors,
harming no one
but the one who wounds me.

I stand up firmly, high and proud
above the bed. My lower part,
somewhere beneath, is shaggy.

Sometimes a fair farmer's daughter
will make a grab, a daring maid
will get a grip on me.

Rushing upon my redness,
ravaging my head, she
sticks me in a dark and secret place.

Before long she will feel the force
of our meeting, the curly-haired
maiden who holds me fast—
her eye will be wet.

Riddle 27

I'm treasured by men, found far and wide
brought forth from forests and fortresses,
hills and vales. By day I'm borne aloft
on wings, carried with care
to a sheltering roof. Then they give me
a bath in a barrel. Now I become
the enslaver and scourge of men,
quickly throwing young heroes to the earth
and sometimes their elders as well.

Whoever feuds with me, setting himself
against my strength, soon finds
that his back will be bouncing on the ground.
Let him talk tough
but unless he repents his foolishness in time
his strength will be stolen, his power sapped.
He will lose control of his hands, his feet, his mind.

Guess what they call me,
who on this earth enslave men so,
leaving them befuddled from my blows
when daylight dawns.

Riddle 44

It hangs in splendor by a man's thigh,
beneath its master's cloak. There's an opening in front.
It's stiff and hard, and finds a fitting home
when the youth lifts his robe above his knees,
hoping to greet with its dangling head
the familiar hole of equal length
he has filled so many times before.

Riddle 5

I'm a lonely wretch, wounded by iron,
bitten by swords. I'm sick and tired
of war-work, weary of blades.
I've seen too much fierce fighting.
No comfort will come, no rescue
from battles between men
until I am utterly destroyed.

The hammer's heirloom hits me
hard-edged and battle-sharp
the smith's handiwork bites.
I will never find a doctor on this field
to heal my wounds with herbs.
So my sword-scars only grow greater
with death-blows day and night.

Riddle 61

Sometimes a lovely lady locks me
up tight in her drawers. Sometimes,
at her dear lord's request,
she teasingly takes me out
and gives him what he's asking for.

Then he sticks his head inside me,
working his way from underneath
up into my narrow place. If the man
who seizes me is strong enough,
my loveliness will soon be filled
with something rough and shaggy.

Tell me what I mean!

Riddle 46

The Queen of Sheba is said to have posed this riddle to Solomon.

A man sat at wine with two wives
two sons and two daughters,
beloved sisters, and their two noble
firstborn sons. The father of each
of those princes was present,
and also the uncle and nephew.
In all, there were five
in the family sitting there.

Riddle 45

I hear tell of something
rising in a corner: growing,
enlarging, raising its roof.
The bride, a prince's daughter
proudly grasps the boneless, swelling thing
and places it under her cloth.

Riddle 47

A moth munching on words—
I thought it something strange and weird
when I heard about that wonder,
how a worm would swallow
the songs of men, a thief in the dark
of our glorious speech
and its firm foundation.

And yet, this larcenous little guest
was not one whit the wiser
for all of the words he devoured.

Riddle 54

The young man came
to the place he knew he'd find her, standing
in the corner. The bold and vigorous youth
stepped up to her and, hefting up
his own robe with his hands,
thrust in something stiff beneath her girdle.

He worked his will upon her
standing there. They trembled
and shook. The thane was in a hurry.
He was up to the job at first,
that willing plowboy, but after a while
grew weary of the work.

Beneath her girdle there began to grow
something men love
and pay good money for.

Answers to Riddles

These riddles do not come with answers, and some in the Exeter Book have still not been solved.

Here are some likely answers—maybe you can come up with even better ones.

25. An onion

27. Honey mead

44. A key

5. A shield

61. A shirt

46. Lot's family

The five (where there should be fifteen) are Lot, his two daughters, and the two sons he had by them.

45. Bread dough

47. A bookworm

54. A butter churn

Beowulf

Episodes

Introduction to *Beowulf*

Beowulf is a *fantastic* poem in every sense of the word. In all of Western literature, perhaps only the *Odyssey* has rooted mythic imagination so securely in solid human reality. Those returning with distant memories from school will be shocked to discover just how *fantastic* it really is—how chilling the drama, how delicious the scene-setting, how engaging the characters.

We think of *Beowulf* as "primitive" because it was written long ago. "Primitive" it is, in arousing primal emotions and seeking out the roots of human hopes and fears. But as literary art it is also highly sophisticated, the product of a great and ancient poetic tradition. And its mingling of two cultures with quite opposite values makes it even more complex than Homer. Written in the "twilight of the gods," as German paganism was giving way to Christianity, we find both worldviews echoing through the high halls of *Beowulf*.

Around the time of *Beowulf*, on the other side of the world, Chinese literature was reaching new heights with a trio of Tang dynasty poets: Wang Wei, Li Po, and Tu Fu. Far from considering *them* as "primitive," the Chinese have always regarded this as the pinnacle of their literary history.

Unlike the famed Chinese trio, the identity of the *Beowulf* poet remains unknown to us. We have only a rough idea when he may have lived, perhaps sometime around AD 800. Who was this anonymous poet, and how did he come to "write" *Beowulf*? "Write" is in quotes because *Beowulf*, like all poetry in the great oral tradition, was probably composed and recited *from memory*, and only written down much later on.

The Oral Tradition

Such feats of memory, involving thousands of lines of verse, seem incredible now, when we rely so much on technology to aid our recollection. In fact, the ancients were full of dire predictions about the first such "technology"—that of writing itself. They feared that writing would weaken our powers and rob the treasure house of human memory—and, as it turned out, they were right.

Thousands of years before writing, all human culture was passed down through the art of poetry, whose patterns of stress and sound made knowledge more memorable. Poetry was the vehicle not only for history and myth, but even grammar, science and mathematics. The poet's mind was our first library, our first university.

How did they do it? One suggestive hint is that Homer, our first-known epic poet, was blind. Such extraordinary powers of inner concentration might come more naturally to one deprived (or, as a blind poet friend used to say, "relieved") of outward vision. Similarly, Irish bards were trained in dark caves or windowless rooms, where they would lie for hours listening to the master bards recite, until at last they could repeat the longest poems after just one hearing.

Our newly fledged bard (or African *griot*, Greek *rhapsode*, Norse *skald*, or Anglo-Saxon *scop*) might find employment in the hall of a king or nobleman. There he would entertain the guests at banquets, reciting poetry and playing the harp, like a singer-songwriter with his guitar. He too would be expected to compose new songs, celebrating the deeds of his lord and his noble companions.

Did he compose like Mozart, who used to create entire symphonies in his head, and only write them down when every note was perfect? Or more like a jazz musician, using a store of memorized phrases or "licks" to improvise on the chords of a standard tune?

The answer was discovered by Milman Parry and Albert Lord. There were hints in Homer, such as the frequent repetition of little phrases like "rose-fingered dawn." Parry and Lord found a living culture of oral poetry in Bosnia, where poets were still reciting and creating poems that rivaled Homer's in length. They created these poems from a large stock of memorized phrases suitable to every metrical need. Surprisingly, even recitals of old poems were fresh acts of creation, with the poet using new phrases to flesh out a well-known plot. They were like jazz musicians, improvising as they went along.

The implications were clear: our written *Iliad* and *Odyssey* are merely recordings of *one* possible performance, which would have varied with each recitation. The ancient Greeks were well aware of this, and took pains to create a "standard" written version with the best from several different *rhapsodes*.

The Building Blocks of Beowulf

The evidence of oral composition is clear in *Beowulf* as well. The most obvious signs are the little standard phrases constantly being inserted next to a name, to fill out the meter of the line. The variations are endless: "the good king," "the brave man," "the staunch hero," "the tough warrior," "the son of (fill in the blank)." These "fillers" are tossed in with more regard to meter and alliteration than to meaning. Hence the Danes are called "brave" and "valiant" at the very times they are being most cowardly, "victorious" when suffering their worst defeat. There is irony here, but it is probably not intentional.

So the scribe or monk who wrote down *Beowulf* may not have been the poet who composed it. Indeed, it may not have been the work of one poet at all, but a *line* of poets gradually elaborating primitive tales into the satisfying and sophisticated work of art we have today.

Only one manuscript of *Beowulf* survives today, copied around AD 1000. We are lucky to have that: it was almost destroyed by a fire that left its edges singed. A photographed edition of the manuscript, published by the Early English Text Society, is widely available and fascinating to peruse.

The Story

Let's pull up a bench in the mead hall, grab a brew, and enjoy a jazzy new performance of that old crowd-pleaser, *Beowulf*. Mead, by the way, is an alcoholic drink made from honey. A little will no doubt improve the poetry—but watch out, or you'll end up like the guys in Riddle 27.

We won't hear all three thousand lines tonight—this tale is "to be continued." In fact, it divides neatly into three episodes, each with a knock-down, drag-out battle. Beowulf himself recaps the action for the benefit of those who missed the previous episode.

Harrumph!

The tale begins with one word, "Hwaet!" No one really knows what it means. Perhaps meant to get the attention of a rowdy crowd, it might be translated as "Listen up!" or, with a properly guttural "Hw," a loud clearing of the throat before beginning. The *scop* plays a lovely little intro on his harp, and off we go.

Bringing us up to speed on the current situation, the poet recounts the mysterious origins of the Danish dynasty. The icy ship-funeral of its founder, Scyld Scefing, is one of the great moments of the poem, forming a pair with Beowulf's funeral pyre at the end.

Enter the Monster

Scyld's great-grandson, Hrothgar, has a problem. To celebrate his triumphs, he has built the greatest hall on earth, named Heorot. But Grendel, an ogre living nearby, is enraged by the singing and shouting that goes on there. (Those with loud, partying neighbors may sympathize.) It's not just the noise: like Satan in the Anglo-Saxon Genesis, this "joyless" creature can't bear the thought of human happiness. He begins killing and eating Hrothgar's warriors, laying the kingdom waste.

Enter the Hero

Beowulf of the Geats (a kingdom in the west of modern Sweden) hears about Hrothgar's troubles. A young man in search of fame and glory, he decides to help out. With a few picked companions he makes the voyage to Denmark. The Danish coast guard (an Old Sarge type) greets these uninvited guests with a proper tongue-lashing, but relents when he hears what they've come for.

The Fight with Grendel

Hrothgar welcomes Beowulf with a great feast, but Unferth, the king's jealous Danish counselor, tries to throw cold water on his reputation. The hero proves he can wrestle with words, at least, as he deftly turns the tables on his accuser. After dinner, the Danes leave Beowulf and his men alone to face the ogre.

Grendel approaches Heorot, in a passage of spine-tingling poetry. Beowulf's men (like the disciples at Gethsemane) have all gone to sleep. Beowulf only pretends to be asleep. He watches carefully as the monster kills and eats one of his men. Such cold-blooded calculation hardly squares with our idea of a hero, but it pays off when the ogre makes a grab for him. Once Grendel feels Beowulf's grip, it's the monster's turn to worry.

Suspense

The Anglo-Saxons had a low tolerance for suspense. Just when things get sticky for the hero (or the heroine in *Judith*), the poet turns to reassure his worried audience. Evidently they preferred artistic foreshadowing to unrelieved anxiety. There is a great deal of suspense, however, in the buildup to each battle. And over the course of the poem there is a larger arc of suspense, as each struggle becomes increasingly difficult and desperate.

Episode Two: The Fight with Grendel's Mother

All is feasting and happiness after Beowulf's victory—until Grendel's mother shows up, looking to avenge her son. She kills Hrothgar's most beloved counselor and flees with his corpse. The poet says she is less fierce than Grendel, being a woman. But Beowulf is about to find out otherwise.

At the eerie lake where she lives, a repentant Unferth gives Beowulf his own sword to fight with. Plunging in with full armor, Beowulf is discovered by Grendel's mother and dragged into her den. Far from being "the weaker sex," she overpowers and nearly kills him with her dagger. Unferth's weapon proves useless, but he slays her with an ancient sword he finds in the den. Its blade melts from her blood.

The Danish kingdom is cleansed at last. Hrothgar sends Beowulf home with gifts and treasure—and manly tears. Even the gruff old coast guard shows his gratitude.

Episode Three: The Fight with the Dragon

Back home in Geatland, Beowulf gives his own king, Hygelac, a good share of the treasure. No longer the strong, silent hero, Beowulf is now relaxed and chatty. Discussing Freawaru's marriage he shows keen insight, explaining how feuds keep flaring up again.

Beowulf eventually becomes king of the Geats. Thanks to astute diplomacy, he reigns peacefully into old age—until a dragon begins to ravage the land. He decides, in a final heroic deed, to fight it single-handed.

He has an iron shield made to ward off the fire, but even this is not enough. His sword breaks in the battle, and he is in agony when Wiglaf, a young warrior, comes to his aid. The two of them kill the dragon, but not before Beowulf is bitten in the neck.

The old king dies of the poison bite, and the Geats grieve as they put the torch to his funeral pyre. His final act, sacrificing himself for his people, is the epitome of both pagan and Christian virtue. They bury Beowulf with songs of praise, in a barrow high above the sea.

The Roots of Beowulf

A lot of fascinating literary archeology has gone into tracing the origins of Beowulf in ancient tales and sagas. One popular story with many variants was "The Bear's Son's Tale," in which an ogre attacks the house of an old king. His youngest son injures the monster, but it escapes. They follow the bloody trail to a strange place where the hero fights a demon (sometimes female).

Interestingly, the name "Beowulf" can be interpreted as "bee-wolf," a metaphor for "bear," an animal that preys on bees for honey. Such little riddles or "kennings" (like "whale-way" for the sea) are one of the delights of Anglo-Saxon poetry.

Tantalizing similarities are also found in the Saga of Hrolf Kraki. Bothvar Bjarki (whose last name means "little bear") is a Geat hero who comes to the court of King Hrolf (our Hrothulf) in Denmark. He slays a monster that has terrorized the Danes. Unfortunately, this saga and the Bear stories were written down much later than Beowulf. But there are hints that all drew on still-earlier stories.

Who Was Grendel?

Remarkably, we feel not only horror, but a very real sympathy for Grendel and his mother. His terror of Beowulf is as real as the Danes' terror of him. And she, after all, is a grieving mother whose son has just been killed:

> Grendel's mother had taken the bloody hand
> she knew so well.
> Sorrow sprang up again—
> it was no happy exchange
> when both sides had to pay
> with a loved one's life.

This is no comic-book portrayal of superheroes and villains: even the monsters here are (almost) human.

If the monsters in *Beowulf* feel real to us, it's because they *were* real to the Anglo-Saxons. The "Maxims" poem, which tells the proper place of things in the Anglo-Saxon world, puts God in his Heaven and the king on his throne—but also the ogre in his fen and the dragon in his cave. The soberly factual Anglo-Saxon Chronicle tells of fiery dragons flying through the sky. *Beowulf* was no fairytale. Nor did they make a distinction, as we do, between its "mythic" and its "historic" elements. It was *all* true history to them.

Whence comes this strange assortment of Germanic trolls and ogres? A life lived close to wolves and bears, surrounded by forest, with no light but fire, may account for much. Fireside tales of larger, more terrible creatures may have filtered down from the distant past, when their ancestors faced cave bears and sabretooth cats. Man was not always the most feared predator in his world.

But the insistence that Grendel was "like a man, but larger" is intriguing. Could there have been some lingering memory of Neanderthal Man, who, for thousands of years, haunted Europe alongside modern humans? Like Grendel, the doomed race would have been crowded out onto less-desirable land, the "swamps and fens," before complete extinction. With a brute strength far greater than ours, they would have been a fearsome enemy.

We can only speculate. But ever since, in song and story, we have been celebrating the victory of intelligence over sheer brute strength. And, as we know, history is written by the victors—who always turn the defeated into monsters.

"What Has Ingeld Got to Do with Christ?"

This was the exasperated complaint of Alcuin, Charlemagne's chief scholar, when he heard about the passion of the English monks for stories of Ingeld and other Germanic heroes. An English monk himself, Alcuin was busy teaching France how to read and write—while back home, his brothers seemed to be reverting to barbarism!

Nothing would change the English love for their heroic heritage—Christianity would just have to get used to it. Pope Gregory took a liberal attitude toward such harmless pastimes among his "angels," creating the climate for a host of pagan-Christian hybrids.

Caedmon and his fellow poets did not simply pour new Christian wine into old German bottles. They infused the heroes—and monsters—of Christianity with a new "barbarian" strength and enthusiasm, a hybrid vigor reflected equally in the Christ of the "Dream of the Rood" and the Satan of Genesis.

Beowulf's unique blend of cultures comes from the opposite direction. Here a pagan hero is endowed with a character that even Christians can admire. Some of the Christian elements are fairly superficial, little pious asides that seem to be tacked on as an afterthought. One can imagine a monk who can't help "improving" the story a bit as he commits it to parchment.

But the Christianity of *Beowulf* goes far deeper. The characters of Beowulf and Hrothgar, while displaying all the old heroic virtues, are deeply infused with qualities of humility and human kindness that would have endeared them even to Alcuin. In the last words of the poem, Beowulf is praised equally for Christian and pagan virtues. Of all the world's kings, he was

> the most kind and gentle,
> most gracious to his people
> and most eager for everlasting fame.

In his final battle with the dragon, his insistence on fighting *alone* is pure pagan heroism. Seen purely in those terms, it might be seen as the hero's typical tragic flaw: *ofermod*, overconfidence leading to defeat, just as we saw with Byrhtnoth at the Battle of Maldon.

But seen in Christian terms, Beowulf is a good shepherd who gives his life for his sheep. He is approaching death anyway, so the terrible risk seems justified. Is it really *ofermod* if you *expect* to die? For the reader there is no doubt that Beowulf is doomed, as the poet makes clear from the beginning. So this final battle becomes a Christ-like sacrifice, fulfilling the highest ideals of both pagan and Christian heroism.

Perhaps the *scops*, playing to an increasingly Christian audience, gradually modified their heroes to make them more agreeable to the new cultural ethos. But they did so with great discretion. Even though the action takes place five hundred years after Christ, there is no mention of Jesus or the Trinity. The Danes and Geats of that time had still not heard of the new religion. They lived in a pre-Christian world that is preserved as carefully in *Beowulf* as the set of a "period" historical drama. Other poets were not so scrupulous: the Old Testament heroine in *Judith*, for instance, prays to a New Testament Trinity of Father, Son, and Holy Spirit.

There are a few "editorial" intrusions by the poet, who is clearly Christian. Attempting to explain the origin of monsters like Grendel, the poet calls them "the race of Cain," cursed by God like their forebear and cast out from human society. Hrothgar is criticized for sacrificing to pagan idols in his desperation to be rid of Grendel—though the poet admits he did not know any better.

Beowulf and Hrothgar could not be Christians. But the *scops* manage, rather brilliantly, to endow them with a kind of natural piety. They do this in part by playing with the Germanic concept of *wyrd*, or fate. Inexorable, inscrutable, by turns kind and cruel, *wyrd* was a force which even the bravest hero bowed to.

It was no great leap from *wyrd* to the stern, demanding deity of the Old Testament. The terms *"wyrd"* and "God" are both used for the arbiter of fate, so that Beowulf's stoic acceptance of *wyrd* is also a humble submission to the will of God. But he also attributes help and comfort to this God, a purely Christian concept. Beowulf emerges as an *anima naturaliter cristiana*, a naturally Christian soul, a pagan one could hope to meet in Heaven.

The Clash of Values

The *scops* had a tougher job trying to square "love thy neighbor" with the Germanic code of honor and vengeance. The Roman historian Tacitus describes this code as a mutual obligation between lord and warrior. The warrior owed his lord absolute loyalty. If his lord fell in battle, he must avenge him at any cost. The lord, in turn, rewarded loyalty and valor with generous gifts. Lords who do not live up to this obligation, like Heremod, are criticized bitterly. Those who do, like Hrothgar and Hygelac, win praise.

And praise was the point of it all. Without much of an afterlife to look forward to, the whole aim of a hero's life was to win fame for valor. This was the only real immortality. Christian humility had no place here. Boasting about past and future deeds was part of the game, especially after a little too much mead. But a man was expected to live up to his mead-hall boasts in battle.

So far so good. Granted, these guys were short on humility, but Christians could get behind virtues like loyalty and courage, honesty and generosity. And indeed *Beowulf* can be seen as an effort by the Anglo-Saxons to affirm the enduring and positive values of their Germanic heritage.

But vengeance was another matter. Too often it was the driving force behind pagan political life. The Christian position was unequivocal: "Vengeance is mine, saith the Lord." At every turn, the poem subverts the pagan code of vengeance, showing over and over the terrible, endless violence it engenders. We suffer with

Hildeburgh, who loses husband, son and brother in the feud at Finnsburg. Beowulf explains how envy and hatred perpetuate the cycle. As the poem closes, his people, deprived of his protection, will be swept up again in this endless tragedy. Vengeance, and not Grendel, is the villain of the poem.

The Players

Beowulf is full of little asides about historical and legendary characters. The audience would have understood these allusions, just as we know what it means to call someone an Einstein or a Benedict Arnold. But we need a program to understand these players—and see what evil lurks behind those smiling faces at the feast.

Legend has it that *Scyld Scefing* arrived on Danish shores as an infant set adrift in a boat. Some say the boat was filled with treasure. A fitting ending, then, to set him adrift at death in another treasure-laden ship. The Danes are called *Scyldings* after him. Scyld's son *Beow* is confusingly called "Beowulf" in the manuscript. This seems to be a mistake; his name appears as "Beow" in historical genealogies.

Sigemund the Volsung was a mythic Norse hero who slew a dragon single-handed. He is compared with Beowulf, who has slain a monster not only single-handed but bare-handed. But there is a darker foreshadowing too—Beowulf will meet his end in combat with a dragon.

The violent and greedy king *Heremod* is contrasted with Beowulf, and mentioned by Hrothgar as a good example—to avoid. Obviously, he made a deep impression on the Danes. Perhaps it was Heremod who left them kingless and miserable at the beginning of the poem, before the coming of Scyld Scefing.

Something Rotten in the State of Denmark

Hrothulf sits next to Hrothgar at the feast. The son of Hrothgar's brother, he could compete with Hrothgar's own sons for the throne. Queen Wealtheow pointedly reminds Hrothulf of all the generous things they've done for him. She is *sure* he will take care of her boys when Hrothgar is gone.

He does, but not as Wealtheow would have wished. Rather than acting as their guardian, Hrothulf seizes the throne for himself. Hrothulf's takeover is so successful, in fact, that history forgets all about Hrothgar. Later, in the *Saga of Hrolf Kraki*, a character similar to Beowulf will come to help king *Hrothulf* instead of Hrothgar.

Women as Weavers of Peace

Women held an honored and powerful position in Anglo-Saxon society, and the women in *Beowulf* are viewed with admiration and sympathy. Queen *Wealtheow* moves through Hrothgar's hall with assurance and self-possession. She gives out gifts of treasure and wields great power. She assures Beowulf that "The warriors who drink here will do as I bid them to." Beowulf tells Hygelac she is a "pledge of peace between nations." Her marriage to Hrothgar, intended to seal an alliance, has evidently been a success, both personally and diplomatically.

But at Hrothgar's feast, the *scop* sings a tragic tale. The "Fight at Finnsburg" involves a Danish princess, *Hildeburh*. She was sent to marry Finn the Frisian as a "peace-weaver" to patch up a feud. But things go terribly wrong, and she loses her husband, son and brother. (See "The Finnsburg Fragment" for more details.)

Back home, Beowulf discusses the upcoming marriage of Hrothgar's daughter, *Freawaru*. The Danes have killed Froda, king of the Heathobards. Now Hrothgar is giving Freawaru as a peace-weaver to Froda's son *Ingeld*. (Yes, this is Alcuin's Ingeld.) Beowulf doubts it will work out any better than it did for Hildeburh.

In contrast with these ladies, *Modthryth* was an evil princess, executing any man who dared to look in her direction. She is sent off (with some relief, no doubt) to marry the dashing young champion *Offa*. Surprisingly, she is transformed by love and they live happily ever after. This "taming of the shrew" may have been thrown in to flatter the English king Offa, namesake of Beowulf's ancient hero. No doubt it won smiles at his court.

Feuding with a Vengeance

Once he is king, Beowulf proves that he is not just a headstrong hero, but a shrewd politician. He achieves brilliant success against the Swedes, revenging his king and placing a friend on the Swedish throne. The story of this longstanding feud is scattered throughout the last episode. Let's set it out in order here.

1. Beowulf's Geats, led by king Hygelac, attack and kill the Swedish king, Ongentheow.

2. Ongentheow's sons, Onela and Othere, fight for the Swedish throne. Onela kills Othere.

3. Othere's sons, Eadgils and Eanmund, flee to the Geats.

4. Hygelac's son Heardred, now king of the Geats, gives them refuge.

5. This angers Onela, the Swedish king, who attacks and kills Heardred.

6. One of Onela's warriors, Weohstan, also kills Eadgils' brother Eanmund (see 3 above).

7. Beowulf becomes king of the Geats.

8. To avenge his former king, Beowulf helps Eadgils (3 above) overthrow the Swedish king Onela.

9. Peace comes at last, with Beowulf's good friend Eadgils on the Swedish throne.

Whew! This Beowulf obviously has brains as well as brawn. Thanks to his patient and subtle diplomacy, the Geats and Swedes enjoy many years of friendship.

But with Beowulf dead, the Geats once again fear the Swedes. Why? Shouldn't their king Eadgils be *grateful* to the Geats, who put him on his throne? Well, yes— but. Remember Wiglaf, the young man who fought the dragon with Beowulf? He is now king of the Geats.

Unfortunately, his father Weohstan (6 above) was the one who killed Eadgils' brother Eanmund. So Eadgils and his Swedes are honor-bound to avenge themselves against Wiglaf and the Geats. The epic ends here, but the poem foreshadows the verdict of history: the Geats' homeland will be overwhelmed by Sweden.

The message is clear. Even if you play it as brilliantly as Beowulf, you just can't win at the game of revenge. No one escapes the tangled web that pagan blood feuds weave.

An interesting footnote to this story is that Geats, perhaps fleeing defeat in Sweden, may have founded one of the earliest English kingdoms. Royal names, and heirlooms found in the Sutton Hoo ship burial, point in that direction. Perhaps it's no accident that the hero of this *English* epic was a *Geat*. When facing misfortune, as poets have always known, writing well is the best revenge.

Translating *Beowulf*

As much as possible, I have aimed to let the poet speak for himself. I have tried to avoid the kind of *over-translation* that turns poetic phrases like "bone-lock" and "life-sick" into prose like "shoulder joint" and "fatally wounded."

Likewise, I have not tried to disguise the repeated formulaic phrases of oral poetry. Modern poets try to avoid common phrases like "safe and sound" or "far and wide." Oral poets, however, relied on such ready-made verbal "bricks" to build their vast poetic structures. And many we still use today come straight from Anglo-Saxon.

In order to remain true as possible to the meaning of the original, I have not tried to imitate its verse form—the reef on which so many have wrecked their ships. Instead I have opted for a flexible line that retains the flavor and, hopefully, the power of alliterative verse.

Since modern English depends on word order for its meaning, rather than the cases and declensions of its Anglo-Saxon ancestor, the translator's first job is to unravel the complexities of Germanic syntax. The old poets called their art "weaving words." The translator, alas, must now *unweave* them, teasing a single skein of meaning from this densely-woven fabric.

Anglo-Saxon offers us the pleasure of rummaging among the roots of our language, and wherever possible I have used modern descendants of Old English words. This is no sacrifice, as Anglo-Saxon root words are short, punchy and powerful. It has been noted that when present-day poets speak from the heart (or the gut), they all speak Anglo-Saxon.

I can honestly say I have enjoyed every minute I have spent with this wonderful poem, and was sad as any Geat to see our hero's funeral pyre. I hope you enjoy it just as much!

Dan Veach
Atlanta, Georgia

Beowulf

Episode One

GRENDEL

Listen! We Spear-Danes
have heard the bygone glory
of our people's kings, how those princes
accomplished such courageous deeds.

Scyld Scefing took the mead benches
from many an enemy host,
striking terror into their troops.
He was first found as an orphan
alone and abandoned, but he grew under heaven
to honor and glory, until neighbors and nations
far over the whale's road obeyed him
sent tribute and treasure. That was a good king!

Later on, a son was born to Scyld,
a youth in the yard, sent by heaven
to comfort his people, who, God knew,
had suffered through terrible times of need
without a leader. The Lord of Life,
the Ruler of Glory gave worldly renown
to Beow, son of Scyld: his fame sprang far
and wide throughout the realm.

A young man should always do
as Beow did—give generous gifts
while under his father's wing
so when he comes of age and faces war
his chosen companions will follow him.
Praiseworthy deeds will profit a man
among people everywhere.

Scyld's funeral ship

When Scyld arrived at his fated hour,
still hale and hearty, he passed
into the keeping of the Lord.
Then his dearest companions
took him down to the edge of the sea
as he had bid them do
while he still wielded words,
the friend of the Scyldings, beloved lord
who had ruled them long.

There in the harbor stood
with a great curved prow
sheathed in ice
and eager to set out,
a ship for a king.

They laid their beloved lord,
the great ring-giver, in the middle
by the mast. Treasure from far-off lands
was loaded on board. I never heard
of a ship decked out so splendidly
with armor and weapons of war, chain mail
and brilliant blades. On his breast they placed
a heap of gold and jewels to carry with him
when the tide took him far out to sea.

His folk gave him from their treasury
no fewer gifts than those people
who, at the outset of his life
cast him adrift, a child
alone on the waves.

They set his golden standard
high overhead, then gave him back
to the ocean, let the waves
bear him away. Hearts were weighed with grief,
spirits mournful. No man can say for sure,
no counselor in the hall,
no hero under heaven,
where that ship bore its cargo.

The line of King Hrothgar

After his father passed away
Beow was the Scyldings' much-loved king
famed among his folk for many years.
After him the great Healfdene,
battle-fierce even when old,
ruled the brilliant Scylding nation.
From him four children are counted,
awakened to this world by that lord of hosts:
Heorogar and Hrothgar
and Halga the good. I've also heard
that his Yrse was Onela's queen
and beloved bed-companion.

To Hrothgar was given good fortune in war
and honor among men, so that his friends
and kinsmen followed him eagerly
and the youth grew into greatness.

Hrothgar builds a great hall

Then an idea entered his mind:
he would command a great mead-hall be built,
one that the sons of men would remember forever.
There he would give out, to young and old
all the great wealth God had granted him,
holding back only the people's land
and the lives of men.

The mighty work was announced to many nations
upon this middle earth, for them to help adorn
the people's dwelling. And quickly, for a work of men,
the greatest of halls was made ready.
The poet, whose words wield power everywhere,
named it "Heorot."

Hrothgar was good as his word—
he dealt out rings and treasure at his table.
The hall soared up high and horn-gabled.
It still awaited the scourge of war and fire,
when the sword-hate of a son-in-law
would someday awaken in slaughter.

An evil awakes

Then a powerful monster,
dwelling in darkness, started to suffer miserably—
day after day he would have to hear
loud laughter and rejoicing in that hall,
the sound of the harp and the clear song
of the poet.

The creation of man
was the story sung so well, how long ago
the Almighty wrought the earth, the bright
and lovely lands embraced by water,
how he set, rejoicing in triumph,
the sun and the moon in their places,
shedding radiant light upon the land-folk,
and then adorned the surface of the world
with limbs and leaves. He created
and quickened every kind of creature
that walks the earth.

And so that noble troop lived days
of joy and ease—until a fiend from Hell
attacked them. The grim thing's name was Grendel,
a huge border-stalker, he ruled the moors
and marshes, fens and fastnesses.
The unblessed being had guarded long
this land of monsters and misshapen things—
ever since God had cursed the race of Cain.

The eternal Lord avenged the murder
of Abel. Cain would get
no satisfaction from that feud.
As retribution for his crime
the Creator drove Cain far from all mankind.
From him would spring all manner
of misbegotten things: ogres and elves
and orc-monsters, likewise the giants
who warred against God for so long
before they got their just reward.

Grendel comes to Heorot

After night had fallen, Grendel stirred
and sought out that high house
where the Ring-Danes, after a bout of beer,
had settled in. There he found the noble troop
sleeping soundly after their feast. Sorrow
and the sad fate of men were all forgot.

Grim and greedy, the evil thing
was suddenly eager now—
with cruel ferocity, he ripped
thirty men from their rest.
Exulting in his booty,
he headed back home
with a bellyfull of slaughter.

In the next dawn's light
Grendel's terrible war-craft was revealed.
Where there had been feasting before,
weeping and screaming rose aloft,
a great cry at morning. The good old king
sat in sorrow, suffering for his thanes.

Nor would they have long to rest—
the next night he was back again
ravaging, murdering even more men.
Grendel had no regret at all
for these terrible atrocities—
he was far too steeped in evil.

After that it wasn't hard to find
those who sought their rest someplace removed,
bedded down in the barns and outbuildings
once the hatred of the new hall-thane
was clear to all. Those who would escape the fiend
held themselves aloof from Heorot.

Grendel's reign of terror

So Grendel ruled and warred against the right,
one against all, until the best of halls
stood empty and deserted.
Twelve long winters the Scylding king
suffered through every kind of woe and grief.

And so it was known through sorrowful songs
to all the sons of men, how Grendel
waged his hateful war on Hrothgar,
assault and outrage season after season
without respite. He would not make peace
with any Dane. Not for any price
could they buy off the bane of their lives.
Nor did any wise man need expect
bright blood-money from this killer's hand.

No, the dark death-shadow
lay in wait to ambush every man,
young brave or grizzled veteran.
He held the misty moors
in endless night. No man knows where
Hell's hidden servants stalk upon their rounds.

The terrible creature who walked alone
committing such crimes against mankind
now dwelt in Heorot, that jeweled hall,
in the dark of night. Still, he never dared
approach the king's gift-seat, the treasure-throne—
he feared it, for he did not know God's mercy.

The Danes call on their gods

All this was a torment to Hrothgar—
it broke his spirit.
Many a time, the ruler sat in council
seeking advice, how best that strong-hearted man
might deal with these shocks and terrors.

Sometimes they ordered sacrifices
in their sacred groves, chanted prayers

to the Demon Slayer, imploring help
against this threat to all their people.
Such was their custom, the hope of the heathens,
remembering Hell in their hearts.
They didn't know their Lord and Maker,
the Judge of all deeds, nor how to praise
the Helm of Heaven, King of Glory.

Woe to him who must, in cruel affliction
thrust his soul into the fire's embrace—
he can hope for neither help nor comfort.
But all will be well with him who,
on his death day, looks to the Lord,
to his Father's embrace for protection.

And so the sorrow of these times seethed endlessly
in the son of Healfdane, nor could the wise man
turn away his troubles. The battle was too hard
and bitter, had lasted too long. For all his nation
this cruel oppression was the worst of nightmares.

Beowulf decides to help Hrothgar

Then to the home of Hygelac's thane
Beowulf, a good man of the Geats
came news of Grendel's deeds.
He was of all mankind the strongest
in that day of this life, great in body
and in spirit.

He ordered a good sea-going ship
be built, saying that he would seek
over the swan-road for that famous lord
and warrior king, since he had need of men.

The wise men did not blame him
for that voyage, though he was dear to them,
but urged on this high-minded man
and watched for omens.

He chose from among the Geats
known champions, the keenest he could find
for this journey. Fifteen altogether
sought out the sea-wood.
Then the current-crafty man
led them down to the shore.

The voyage to Denmark

The time had come. The boat rode
on the waves beneath the cliffs.
Men quickly mounted the prow
as the tide turned, churning up the sand.
Bright treasure they stowed
in the ship's bosom, splendid war-gear.
Then they eagerly shoved off
in that well-bound wood.

Urged on by the wind, the foam-necked ship
sailed like a seabird across the waves.
In good time, on the second day
the curved prow came in sight of land—
broad headlands, steep and shining sea-cliffs.
The ocean crossing was over, the sea journey at an end.

The Storm-Geats jumped out of the ship
and stood on solid land again.
Chain mail war-shirts ringing,
they tied down the boat and gave thanks to God
that their path on the waves had been easy.

The coast guard

Then from a wall the Scylding watchman
whose job was to guard those sea-cliffs
saw them bearing their bright shields
down the gangplank. His mind was on fire
to know what sort of men these were.
This thane of Hrothgar quickly mounted horse
and galloped down to the shore.

He shook his mighty spear with authority
and addressed them in formal words:
"Who are you, carrying arms
and clad in chain mail
who over the sea-roads in this towering ship
come hither on the waves?

"Many a year have I served as coast guard,
watched over the ocean, that no enemy ships
should ever harm this Danish land.
But never have warriors bearing shields
landed so openly without our leave,
without the permission of our people.

"I have never seen a mightier man on earth
than this one of yours in his war-gear—
no mere hall-thane honored to bear arms,
unless his peerless look belies him.

"Now, I need to know your nation and your kin
before you fare farther in this Danish land—
otherwise, you'll be taken for spies.
Listen up, seafarers from some far-off land!
What I have to say is simple:
The sooner you tell me where you're from
the better things will be for you."

Beowulf answers the challenge

The leader of the troop gave answer,
unlocking his word-hoard:
"We are men of the race of Geats,
the hearth-companions of Hygelac.
My father was renowned among this nation,
a noble leader by the name of Ecgtheow,
who endured many winters before he went,
an old man, from our midst. Wise men everywhere
on this wide earth remember him.

"With friendly intentions we seek your king,
the son of Healfdane, shelter of his people.
We are on a great mission
to the famed lord of the Danes.
Guide us well!

"Nor is there any need I know of
to keep it a secret: If what we hear tell
is true, some enemy of the Scyldings—
I don't know what—some secret evil
rules the dark nights with terror,
inflicting unheard-of shame and slaughter.

"I can give Hrothgar good council,
out of a spirit of generosity,
on how that good old man
can overcome his foe—
if his fortune is ever to turn around,
a remedy come for his many afflictions
and the waves of care grow cool.
If not, he'll endure this distress
forever, as long as the best of houses
still stands on high."

The coast guard decides

The coast guard, fearless officer
still seated on his horse, spoke out:
"A sharp shield-bearer must always keep in mind
the difference between words and deeds.
From what I've heard, I deem this troop
is loyal to our Danish lord.
You can go forward, bearing your weapons
and war-gear. I will show the way.

"Likewise, my men will guard your ship
where it sits, freshly tarred upon the sand,
against all enemies. It will be our honor
to hold it until that curved wood prow
bears its beloved men back over the sea
to your Weder land—those courageous ones
who come through the clash of battle."

So they set out on their journey
leaving the broad-beamed ship
resting on its ropes, held fast by its anchor.
Boar crests glittered on helms gold-crusted,
hardened by fire, each one grimly guarding
a fierce warrior's life.

The troop hurried onward eagerly
until they could make out the timbered hall,
stately and glimmering with gold,
the greatest building made by men
under heaven, the ruler's house,
whose radiance shone over many lands.

The guard pointed out that bright home
of brave men. They could see the way.
Then he turned his horse around and said,
"Time to go. It's back to the sea
for me now, to guard against enemy troops.
May the Almighty Father guard you with his grace
and keep you safe in your adventures!"

Hrothgar's hall

The street was handsomely paved
with stone. Their armor shone—
hard, hand-locked rings of iron
glittered and sang in their shirts of mail
as they marched up to the hall in their fearsome gear.

They set their wide, sea-weary shields
against the wall and sank down on a bench,
their chain-mail clinking. The seamen's spears
stood all together, ashwood shafts tipped with gray.
This iron band was well equipped with weapons.

Then a proud warrior questioned the troop:
"Where do you come from with those fancy shields,
grim helmets, gray hauberks, and this heap
of war-shafts? I am Hrothgar's herald
and attendant. I've never seen a braver bunch
of foreigners. Too proud to be exiles, I would guess.
It seems you've sought out Hrothgar in high spirits!"

The Weder lord, famed for courage,
a hard man under his helmet, answered him:
"We are Hygelac's table-companions.
Beowulf is my name.
I wish to tell the son of Healfdane,
your great lord, my errand
if the gracious king will grant it."

Wulfgar replied—a prince of the Wendels
whose spirit, wisdom and valor
were widely known—"As you request,
I will ask the lord of the Scyldings,
friend and ring-giver of the Danes,
about your errand, and shortly bring
the answer that great man sees fit to give."

Quickly he turned back toward the palace
where Hrothgar sat, gray and old, among his nobles.
Boldly he advanced and stood before the Danish king
in accordance with the customs of the court.
Then Wulfgar spoke to his friendly lord:

"We have some travelers here, come from far
across the ocean. They are Geats, and their leader
is a man named Beowulf. They ask, my lord
to exchange a word with you. Please don't deny them
your conversation, gracious Hrothgar.
By their war-trappings, they seem worthy
of high esteem, and the leader who brought them here
is formidable indeed!"

Hrothgar remembers

Hrothgar, helm of the Scyldings, spoke:
"Ah, yes. I knew him as a child.
Ecgtheow was his father's name.
Hrethel, king of the Geats, gave his only daughter
to his house. It is his son now
who comes here on serious business
looking for a loyal friend.

"The seamen who carried gifts
of treasure for the Geats
say he has the strength of thirty men
in the grip of his hand. Holy God
has sent him—such is my hope—
as a gift of mercy to the Danes
against the terror of Grendel.

"I will give the good man treasure
for his courage. Quick—
bid them come in, the whole band
of comrades, and bid them welcome
to the Danish nation."

Wulfgar then went to the door
bringing word from within:
"The victorious lord of the Danes
bids me to say that he knows
your noble lineage, and these brave men
come hither over the sea waves
are welcome here. Now you may enter,
wearing your helmets and battle gear,
to see king Hrothgar. Your shields
and spears will stay outside,
awaiting the outcome of your talk."

Beowulf salutes Hrothgar

The man and his mighty troop of thanes
arose now. Some stayed behind to guard the weapons
as he ordered. The rest quickly followed,
their lord in the lead, under the high roof
of Heorot. Hard under helmet, he advanced
until he stood upon the hearth.
Beowulf spoke, his chain mail shining,
ringed armor sewn by the smith's skillful craft:

"May you be hale and well, Hrothgar!
I am Hygelac's thane and kinsman. I have done
many a glorious deed in my youth.
This thing with Grendel was made known to me
in my native land—the seafarers told us

that this best of halls stood idle,
useless to any man,
after the glow of heaven's evening light
lies hidden.

"The best and wisest among my people
advised me to seek you out, lord Hrothgar.
They had seen for themselves my strength
and skill, seen my armor stained with the blood
of enemies, how I bound and destroyed the five giants,
and at night, in peril on the waves,
slew the sea dragons and avenged the Weders.
I ground up those grim and terrible foes—
they went looking for trouble,
and they found it.

Beowulf's request

"And now I am looking for a meeting,
alone, with the monster Grendel.
King of the Bright-Danes, I have only one favor
to ask you. Defender of warriors, friend
of your folk, now that I have come so far,
please don't deny me this—that I alone,
with my troop of hardened soldiers,
be allowed to cleanse this hall of Heorot.

"Now, I have heard that this monster
in his recklessness, never uses weapons.
And so, to better please lord Hygelac,
I too shall renounce them—I will bear no sword,
no broad yellow shield into battle,
but come to grips with him bare-handed,
foe against foe, in a fight for our lives.
Whoever death takes will have to trust
to the judgment of God.

"If Grendel wins… well, I guess
he will eat Geats as well as Danes.
No need to cover my head with cloth
if he covers me with gore. No,
he will bear off my bloody corpse

for feasting—the lone stalker
will gnaw it without remorse,
staining his swampy retreat.
You won't have to worry for long
about what to do with my body.

"But please send Hygelac, if battle takes me,
this best of war-shirts, which now protects my chest.
The finest of chain-mail garments, it's an heirloom
from Hrethel, and the work of Weland.
Fate will always go the way it must."

Hrothgar's reply

Hrothgar, helm of the Scyldings, spoke:
"Beowulf, my friend, you have sought us out
both for our past deeds, and from your kindness.
Your father, in the greatest of feuds
struck down and slew Heatholaf
in hand-to-hand combat.
Then his Weder kinsmen, for fear of war,
refused to harbor him. He fled
over the rolling waves to the Danish folk,
the Honor-Scyldings.

"That was back when I first ruled
the Danish people in my youth,
that broad realm, stronghold of heroes.
Heregar had died, my older brother,
son of Healfdane—
he was a better man than I was!

"After I settled your father's feud with money,
sent the Wylfings ancient treasures
across the water, he swore allegiance to me.

"It hurts my heart to tell any man
the harm Grendel's hateful attacks
have done me in Heorot. My household troop,
my war-band, has been gutted, swept away
in Grendel's terror. God could so easily put an end
to the crimes of that crazed killer!

"So many times have drunken soldiers
boasted over their mead
that they would abide in the beer-hall,
meet Grendel's attack with their terrible swords.
Then, at morning-tide,
the mead-hall would be decked with gore.
The light of day would show
the horrors of battle in the hall,
the floor beneath the benches soaked with blood.
And I would have the fewer loyal men,
my dear retainers wrenched away by death.

"But now, sit down and feast with us.
Untie your thoughts,
tell us all about your famous deeds
whenever the spirit urges."

Hospitality in Heorot

A bench was cleared in the beer-hall
and the stout-hearted Geats, famed
for strength, sat there together.
A thane did his duty,
brought the jeweled ale-cup
and poured the bright liquid.
The poet raised a clear song over Heorot.
There was joy among the men then,
no small host of Danes and Weders.

Unferth heaps scorn on Beowulf

Then Unferth, Ecglaf's son,
who sat at the feet of the Scylding lord,
spoke up, unleashing his hidden spite.
Beowulf's brave sea journey
caused him great chagrin—
he could never admit that any other man
upon this middle earth or under heaven
could do more glorious deeds than he himself.

"Are you that Beowulf who strove with Breca
over the wide sea in a swimming match?

Proudly flung yourselves into the flood
and, because of some crazy boast,
risked your necks in deep waters?
No man, neither friend nor foe
could talk you out of that sorry stunt.
So you went paddling out on the ocean
embracing the rushing current in your arms
measuring the sea-roads, thrashing with your hands
sliding over the surging waves, the wintry swell.

"For seven nights you both struggled
in the water's grip. But he beat you at swimming—
he was stronger than you were. The next sunrise
the sea would throw him up at Heatho-Raemes.
From there he sought his own dear land of Brondinga
where he had people, towns and treasure.
That son of Beanstan fulfilled his boast against you.

"And so I expect the worst for you,
though you've always come through
in the grim rush of battle, if you dare
to wait here all night long for Grendel."

Beowulf's fight with the sea beasts

Beowulf, son of Ecgtheow, spoke:
"Well, Unferth, my beer-drunk friend,
you certainly have a lot to say
about Breca and his exploits!
But here's the truth—
I had more sea-strength
to strive against the waves
Than any other man.

"The two of us—we were just youngsters then—
boasted we would risk our lives at sea,
and that's exactly what we did.
As we thrashed through the surf
each of us carried a naked sword
gripped hard in hand, to defend ourselves
against the whale-fish.

"Breca was no faster over the floodways,
couldn't distance himself one whit from me,
and I had no intention of leaving him.
Five nights we swam together, until at last
the surging flood forced us apart—
as night darkened, in the freezing weather
the north wind turned fierce
and the waves began to rage.

"Now the sea creatures' anger was aroused.
Against these enemies, my chain mail,
hard and hand-locked, came in handy—
that woven war-shirt, worked with gold,
protected my chest. But something horrible
grabbed me fast in a grim, tight grip
and dragged me to the bottom.

"However, it was granted me
to reach that ogre with my sword—
the mighty sea-beast in his battle-rush
perished at my hand. Over and over
those enraged attackers pressed me hard.
I served them a bellyfull of my noble blade,
as befit such guests. But those man-eaters
never had the pleasure of eating me,
getting their fill of flesh
as they sat upon the sea-floor at their feast.

"Instead, on the morning tide they floated
among the sea drift, put to sleep by the sword.
Never again would these scourges of the ocean
hinder a crossing of that deep ford.

"Light came from the east, God's bright beacon.
The waves calmed down so I could see the headlands,
their wind-swept walls. Fortune often favors
the man whose time has not yet come
if he can keep his courage up!

"In the end, it was granted me to slay
nine of those sea-monsters with my sword.
I've never heard of a harder night's struggle

under heaven's arch, nor a man
in a worse plight on the ocean's pathways.
Still, I escaped the clutches of my foes
and came through it all exhausted but alive.
The sea bore me at last on its swelling waves
and currents to the country of the Finns.

He turns on Unferth

"Now, I've never heard tell about *you*
such sword-terror and dangerous struggle.
Neither you nor Breca in your battle-play
have done anything bold as this
with your fancy swords—not to boast
too much about the matter.

"On the other hand,
you *did* kill your very own brothers,
your closest kinsmen—for that you'll suffer damnation
in Hell, no matter how clever you are.

"I tell you the truth, son of Ecglaf:
Grendel would never have gotten away
with so many crimes against your master,
humiliating him in Heorot, if you
were as fierce a fighter as you think you are.

"But he has learned there's not much need
to fear a feud with you, a sword-storm
from the Victory-Scyldings. He carries
your people off by force, sparing no one,
killing and destroying as he pleases,
expecting no resistance from the Spear-Danes.

"But before long now
the strength and courage of the Geats
will give him a battle.
Anyone who wishes
can go lighthearted to his mead
tomorrow, when the morning light,
robed in brilliance, shines from the south
upon the sons of men!"

Then the treasure-giver was filled with joy.
Gray-haired and famed in battle,
the defender of the Bright-Danes now believed
that help had come, seeing the firm resolve
of Beowulf.

Queen Wealtheow makes a toast and greets her guests

Now there was laughter among the heroes, a pleasant din
of happy conversation rose. Hrothgar's queen
Wealtheow, adorned with gold, came forward
greeting the hall's guests courteously. The noble lady
first gave the Danish king a brimming cup
bidding her beloved lord be blithe
at this beer-drinking. With a will, he took
to the hall-cup and the feast, that famous king.

The lady of the Helmings went about
sharing the jewel-encrusted cup
with veterans and youths
until in due time the queen,
a beautiful spirit adorned with golden rings,
brought the cup of mead to Beowulf.

She greeted the lord of the Geats
and gave thanks to God in wisely-chosen words
that her wish had finally come to pass
that someone would come
to help them in their afflictions.

Beowulf's vow to Wealtheow

The fierce warrior took the full cup
from Wealtheow's hand.
Eager for battle now, Beowulf
Ecgtheow's son, spoke out:

"I made up my mind
when I was out on the ocean
sitting in that sea-boat with my troops
that I would once and for all
fulfill the wishes of your people

or crumple in battle, held fast
in my enemy's grip.
I will accomplish this heroic deed
or else my days will end here in this hall!"

The lady was well pleased with these words,
the Geat's proud boast. Golden-gowned,
the people's noble queen
went to sit by her lord.

Then it was like the old days in the hall—
Joy and gladness reigned again,
noble words were spoken, clamor rose
from a proud and happy people.

Hrothgar leaves the hall to Beowulf

At last the son of Healfdane
sought his evening rest. He knew
the monster had been planning to attack
since they had seen the sun's first light
until the night had darkened over all,
its shadow-helmed shapes come gliding
black beneath the clouds.

The company all arose.
Hrothgar saluted Beowulf, man to man,
wishing him the best and giving him
authority over the wine-hall with these words:

"Never before,
not since I could lift a shield,
have I entrusted the Danes' great hall to any man
as I do now to you.

"Have and hold this best of halls—
set your mind on glory, show your strength and valor,
keep a vigilant watch for the enemy!
You'll never lack for anything you want
if you come through this work of courage
with your life."

Then Hrothgar, bulwark of the Scyldings,
together with his noble warriors, left the hall.
The war chief went to seek queen Wealtheow
in bed.

Beowulf prepares himself

The King of Glory, as men would learn,
had appointed this hall-guard against Grendel.
His extraordinary duty to the Danish king
was keeping watch against the giant. The Geat lord
firmly trusted his strength and spirit
and the grace of God.

Then he took off his iron-mail shirt
removed the helmet from his head
and handed his ornamented sword,
the best of blades, to his serving thane,
ordering him to guard his battle gear.
Then Beowulf spoke a few last words
before he went to bed:

"I don't consider my fighting strength,
my battle-work, as any less than Grendel's.
Therefore my sword will not put him to sleep,
cut off his life—though I could do it if I would.
As brave as he may be in works of evil,
he wouldn't know how best to strike me,
how he might hew down my shield.

So tonight we will forgo the sword
if he dare seek a fight without weapons.
May the all-wise God award glory
to whichever hand the holy Lord
thinks best."

Then the brave warrior lay down,
the pillow receiving his face, and all around
many bold seamen settled down to rest.
Not one of them thought
they would ever see the beloved land

where they grew up, their folk and fortresses, again.
They had heard the rumors: death by slaughter
had taken far too many of the Danish people
in that very hall.

But the Lord was weaving a different destiny
for the Weders: help and comfort
and luck in battle, so that all
might overcome the enemy
through one man's strength and craft.
Truly it is told that mighty God
has always ruled the race of men.

Grendel returns to Heorot

In the black night
the shadow-walker moved softly.
The warriors, who should have guarded
the high hall, slept.
All but one.

All men knew
that unless it were the will of God
no demon could drag them into the shadows.

Still, one man stayed awake
filled with wrath against the foe
fiercely awaiting the outcome of the battle.

Then from the moors and the misty crags
Grendel came stalking. God's wrath was upon him.
The man-eater meant to waylay some warrior
in the high hall. He crept through the clouds
to that place of wine and treasure
sheathed in beaten gold. He knew it well—
it was not the first time
he had sought out Hrothgar's home.
But never, in all his life's days,
would his luck—or the hall-thanes—be harder.

The joyless creature came to the house of men.
In a rage, he tore through the iron-bound door,
ripped open the building's mouth.
Now his tread fell on the inlaid floor.
Heart filled with anger, from his eyes there gleamed,
like fire, an unlovely light.

He saw a host of men before him,
a band of warriors and kinsmen
all asleep. Then his heart laughed—
before the sun rose he meant to tear
each and every life out of its body.
Tonight, the fiend thought,
he would get his fill.

But after this night, fate
was not to let him go on feasting
on the meat of men.
Hygelac's powerful kinsman
was watching him carefully
to see how the creature
would launch his attack.

Without delay, the monster seized
on a sleeping man, ripped him open
without resistance, bit through his joints,
drank the blood from his veins, and bolted
his flesh in huge, horrible chunks.
Before long the dead man had disappeared
right down to his hands and feet.

The fight with Grendel

Now the creature began to creep closer,
reaching out with his claw. Suddenly
he clutched at the stout-hearted warrior
lying still on his bed.

Beowulf sat bolt upright
quickly grabbed hold of the evil thing
and set his weight against its arm.

That master of murder now realized
he had never met, on this middle earth,
the grip of a stronger hand.

Heart-fear for his life now filled him,
but he couldn't shake free.
He was in a panic to be out of there,
running back to his lair, his devil's den.
He had never been in such a fix before.

Then Beowulf remembered all the boasts
he had spoken that evening. Now he stood upright
and tightened his grip. Finger bones burst—
the ogre fought to get free
but the warrior stayed with him.

The nightmare creature was wild to escape
whichever way, flee back to the fens,
but he could feel that the strength of his fingers
was in his grim enemy's grip. It was a hard trip
he had made to Heorot.

A mighty uproar broke out in the mead-hall—
the brave Danes listened in wonder to the din
of that furious drinking-bout. The building
rang out with the rage of the combatants.
It was a wonder the wine-hall could withstand
the two terrible warriors, that the beautiful building
did not crumple and fall to the ground—
but it was held fast, inside and out, by iron bands,
the blacksmith's cunning craftsmanship.

The mead benches, inlaid with gold,
so I hear tell, bent and bounced
from the floor as the enemies grappled.
No Scylding would have thought before
that this splendid horned hall could be broken
by any craft, unless it should be swallowed up
in the hot embrace of fire.

Now a sound rose higher, sending chills of horror
through every North-Dane around the wall
who heard that wail—it was the enemy of God
singing a terrible song, that hell-slave
screaming in his pain. He was held fast
by the man whose might was greatest
in that day of this life.

The defender of men would not for anything
let go of his murderous guest alive—
a life no good to anyone. Beowulf's men
now brandished their ancient blades
trying to defend their famous lord.

What they didn't know, those hardened warriors
hacking away on every side, seeking the monster's soul
was that no iron sword on earth, however sharp,
could touch him—he had cast a spell
that made him safe from any weapon's edge.

But the parting of his soul
from that day of this life
would be a sorry one—
that strange spirit would journey far
into the fiends' kingdom.

He now realized, whose hate for God,
whose crimes had caused mankind such grief,
that his mortal form would fail him.
Hygelac's courageous kinsman
had him by the hand. Each one's life
was hateful to the other.

The terror-monster's body screamed with pain.
A great, gaping wound tore his shoulder—

the sinews sprang apart
and the bone-lock burst.

Beowulf was granted glory
in the battle. Life-sick, Grendel fled
back the fens, his joyless lair.

He knew that he was coming to his end.
The count of his days was complete.

The dream of every Dane
had now come true—this man who came
from a far-off country, courageous and wise,
had cleansed Hrothgar's hall of its curse.

Beowulf rejoiced in his night's work.
The man of the Geats had made good his boast,
saved the Danes from their evil affliction,
the dire need they had endured so long.

As a clear sign that the battle-beast
had given up his arm from hand to shoulder
Grendel's claw was nailed up high
beneath the vaulted roof.

Next day, they go after Grendel

That morning, so I have heard,
the gift-hall was crowded with warriors,
chieftains from far and near, all come
to gaze at that wonder and follow
the monster's tracks. His parting
from this life made no man sorry
as they followed his unhappy path, the way
that weary spirit, wrecked in battle, doomed
by fate, had fled with bloody footprints
to the water-monsters' mere.

The water welled and boiled
with blood, heaving up horrible waves
of hot battle-gore. Doomed to death,
Grendel had hidden here amid the fens.
Without joy, he gave up his heathen soul—
Hell seized him there.

Grizzled veterans and young braves alike
returned from that trip on spirited mounts
rejoicing, shouting their praise for Beowulf aloud.
Many a man said that north or south
nowhere between the seas under heaven's vault
lived there a better man to rule a kingdom.
And this was not to disparage their lord and friend,
the gracious Hrothgar, for he was a very good king.

Sometimes the brave troop let their horses
leap and prance, racing their bay steeds
over the fair paths they knew best.

The poet sings of Beowulf and Sigemund

Then the king's thane, a great speaker
who remembered the old songs and stories
began weaving new words,
tying them together truthfully,
skillfully singing a brand new tale
of Beowulf and his heroic deed.

This called to mind the feats of Sigemund,
so he also sang what he had heard
of that Volsung's journeys,
the marvelous deeds, the crimes and feuds
no man's son knew of but Fitela:
Sigemund always confided in him
as uncle to nephew. Friends in need and in battle,
the two had killed ogres of every kind
with their sharp swords' edges.

After his death day, no small fame
sprang up for Sigemund, when men heard
how that daring warrior killed the dragon,
guardian of the treasure hoard.
Beneath the gray stones that prince's son
had risked the fearful thing alone—
not even Fitela was with him.

But it was granted that his noble blade
should pierce clean through those splendid scales

and stick fast in the wall beyond—
a murderous death blow to the dragon.

The courage of that fearsome warrior
had made the dragon's hoard of rings his own.
The Volsung loaded up a sea-boat,
bore the bright treasure off aboard a ship.
The dragon melted in its own fire.

Sigemund became the most famed of men
for brave adventure. He rose to those heights
after Heremod declined in strength and daring.

King Heremod is contrasted with both heroes

Heremod ended up being betrayed
into the hands of the Jutes, his enemies,
his life quickly extinguished. Too long
had his people been oppressed, overwhelmed
by his troubles and sorrows. His rule
was a lifelong affliction to his nation.

Many a wise man mourned the ways
of that headstrong ruler, who they hoped
would take his father's throne and thrive:
remedy his country's ills, protect his people,
towns and treasure, rule the Scylding's land.
Beowulf was such a man,
a gracious friend to all humanity.
But Heremod had been possessed by evil.

Back at Heorot, Hrothgar rejoices

Racing from time to time, the horses
paced out the sandy paths
as morning light leapt upward.
Stout-hearted retainers from all around
gathered to see the terrible wonder
hung in that high hall.

So too the king himself,
keeper of the ring-hoard, came
from his bride-chamber, stepping
the mead-hall path in triumph
attended by a troop of his best men
the queen and all her maidens right beside him.

Hrothgar stood on the hall steps, gazing
at the steep roof with its hammered gold—
and Grendel's claw.
                    "For this sight,
let us thank the Almighty here and now!
I've suffered many attacks, much grief
from Grendel, but God works wonder
after wonder, the Shepherd of this world.
Not long ago, I thought there was no help
on this wide earth for all my troubles,
when this best of halls was stained with blood
and battle-gore.

"It was a bitter burden for every man—
no one knew how we would ever
defend the stronghold of this nation
from devils and demons.

"Now, through the good Lord's might, this man
has done a deed that went beyond
our wisdom and devising. Well,
the woman who bore this son,
brought him into the race of men,
if she is still alive can truly say
that God was gracious at her giving birth.

"Now Beowulf, best of men
I will love you as a son
for the rest of my life.
Cherish this new kinship—
never shall you want for anything
in this world that is in my power.

"Many times I've given gifts
for less, rewarded weaker warriors.

But as for you, and for this deed,
your fame will live forever.
May the Almighty bring you good,
as He has done already!"

Beowulf gives a modest account

Beowulf, the son of Ecgtheow, spoke:
"It was our pleasure to take on
this work of valor, to risk our lives
against that uncanny power—but how I wish
you could have seen him for yourself,
the fallen fiend in all his glory!

"Hard and fast I clamped him,
hoping I could bind him to his deathbed,
force him to lie there fighting for his life
in my hard handgrip. But it was not
God's will to keep him there—
no matter how desperately I held on
to that deadly foe, he was too strong
to keep from escaping.

"However, he left behind this hand
to guard his retreat—along with his whole arm
and shoulder. The wretched creature
will find little comfort in his flight.
Tormented by sin, tied in the tightening grip
of pain's deadly binds, he won't live for long.
There, stained by crime, he must await
the great Judgment to see what sentence
God in his glory will give him."

Unferth ponders the claw

Unferth son of Ecglaf
was strangely silent now.
He was a quieter man,
less inclined to boast about his war-work,
ever since the court had seen that hand
displayed high overhead, the fiend's fingers
nailed there by that noble man's craft.

At the tip of each finger, hard as steel,
curled the heathen warrior's talons,
an uncanny meat hook.
Everyone said no tempered blade
could touch it, no iron tried and true
could harm the monster's bloody battle arm.

Celebrations in Heorot

Quickly the order went out for hands
to decorate Heorot's interior again.
Many men and women bustled about
getting the guest-hall ready.
Gold-threaded tapestries sparkled on the walls,
a wondrous sight for all who gazed upon them.

The bright house had been badly broken.
The inside was held fast by iron bands
but the hinges had been sprung apart—
only the roof remained completely sound
when the monster, stained by crime,
turned and fled in despair for his life.

But it is not so easy to flee—let him try it who will.
Compelled by necessity, the children of men,
all who bear a soul and dwell on earth,
must seek at last the place that has been prepared,
where the body that covers them, fast in its deathbed,
sleeps after the feast.

Now was the time and place for Healfdane's son
to make his entrance in the hall.
The king was ready to enjoy this banquet.
I've never heard of a larger gathering
or one that bore itself more nobly
around their treasure-giver. This glorious host
bent to the benches and enjoyed their fill.
Hrothgar and Hrothulf, those high-minded men
graciously drank their cupss of mead
in the high hall. Heorot was filled with friends—
there was no secret spite among the Scyldings then.

The son of Healfdane gave to Beowulf,
as reward for his victory, a golden staff
with embroidered battle banner,
a helmet and a chain mail corselet,
and a glorious treasure-sword. Many watched
as they bore the gifts before him. Beowulf
drank a full cup on the mead-hall floor.
No shame in getting gifts like these
in front of all the warriors!

I haven't heard of many men who gave,
among the mead benches, four such gifts
of friendship as these gold-encrusted treasures.

Around the helmet's crest
was a head-guard of woven wire
securely fixed: no forged,
file-sharpened sword could harm it
when a bold man bore his shield
against grim warriors.

The defender of men then ordered eight horses,
each with cheek-pieces of plated gold,
brought into the building, onto the floor of the hall.
One had a saddle cunningly crafted
and adorned with jewels—it was the battle throne
of the high king himself, whenever the son of Healfdane
engaged in swordplay. He never failed on the front lines,
that famous man, when the slaughtered were falling.

So Hrothgar, defender of the friends of Ing,
gave Beowulf horses and weapons
and bade him enjoy them well.
So manfully had this ruler of renown,
keeper of the treasure hoard, rewarded
the rush of battle with rich gifts and horses
that no man who cares to speak the truth
could find any fault with him.

On top of this, he gave heirlooms and treasures
to each man on the mead-bench who had crossed the sea
with Beowulf. He gave gold as well
for the one man killed by Grendel—
he would have killed far more, had not God's wisdom
and man's courage prevented that fate.

The Creator has always ruled mankind
as He does to this day. Therefore, understanding
and foresight of spirit are everywhere best.
Much of love and hate will he endure
who long enjoys days of struggle in this world.

Music and song struck up together
in front of Hrothgar, Healfdane's battle chief.
Plucking the harp's joyful wood
Hrothgar's poet chanted many a song
to entertain the hall.

Then from his mead-bench he began
to recite the song of the sons of Finn—
how a sudden raid struck them
and Hnaef, the hero of the Scyldings
had to fall on a Frisian battlefield.

The Fight at Finnsburg

Hildeburh had little reason
to praise the good faith of the Frisians:
through no fault of her own she was bereft
of those she loved, both son and brother
fated in the clash of shields
to fall pierced by the spear.
That was a grief-stricken lady.

The daughter of Hoc had every reason
to mourn her fate when morning came
and she could see, beneath the sky,
the murderous slaughter of her family,
her greatest earthly joy.

But the battle had also carried off
all of Finn's thanes but a few.
He could not press home
the fight against Hengest in that meeting hall,
drive the thane of the Danish king
and his sad survivors out by force.

So instead Finn offered them terms:
the Frisians would clear another room,
a hall with its own high throne
where they would share power with the Frisians.
Each day Finn, Folcwalda's son, would come
and honor Hengest's troop of Danes
with rings and gifts of gold-encrusted treasure—
just as much as he gave the Frisians
to make them joyful in the beer-hall.

Both sides agreed to a treaty of peace.
Finn swore solemn oaths to Hengest
that he, upon the authority of his council,
would rule the survivors with honor.
Nor would any man by words or works
ever break this agreement
nor even mention it with malice.

Although, being lordless now,
they were forced to follow the killer of their king,
if any Frisian spoke to them scornfully
reminding them of that murderous quarrel
then the sword's edge would settle things.

The funeral pyre was prepared,
gold heaped upon it from the hoard.
The Battle-Scyldings' best warrior,
Hnaef was ready for the fire.
On the pall, blood-stained armor
was piled up everywhere: golden boar-crests, iron-hard.
Many great nobles, gashed by wounds
had fallen in the slaughter.

Hildeburh ordered that her dead son
be placed on the pyre with Hnaef,
committed to the flames, the flesh on his bones
to be burned at his uncle's shoulder.

The princess grieved, gave voice
to a song of sorrow.
The warriors were lifted up.
The greatest of funeral pyres
roared in front of the burial mound
and rolled toward the clouds.

Skulls melted, gashes burst apart,
blood sprang forth again
from the body's cruel bites.
Fire, the greediest spirit,
swallowed them all,
those on both sides taken by the battle,
their glory now gone.

Finn's warriors, bereft of their friends,
returned to homes and forts in Frisland.
Hengest and his Danes stayed with Finn
that whole slaughter-stained winter,
wretched and longing for their land.
But they could not set their ship's curved prow
to sea—the ocean surged with storms,
fought with the wind; winter locked the waves
in bonds of ice.

Another year came to the courtyards,
bringing, as it still does in its proper season,
bright and glorious weather. Winter waned,
the lap of earth grew lush again. The exiled guest
was eager to go.

But his thoughts were more on vengeance
than on voyaging. He longed for one more
bitter meeting, where he could remind the Frisians
of his sword. So he did not refuse his troop's advice
when they placed the sword Hunlafing,
best of blades, the torch of battle, in his lap.
Its edge was well known to the Frisians.

So Finn would face that baleful sword
here in his own house. Guthlaf and Oslaf
complained of his grim attack
after their sea-voyage, bitterly blamed him
for the misery they shared. The Danes
could contain their hearts no longer.

Then the hall was hung with blood and gore
of enemies—Finn was slain
in the midst of his men, his queen
carried away. The Scylding soldiers took
whatever they could find from Finn's house,
furnishings and finely-crafted jewelry.
And they carried their noble lady over the sea
to Denmark, brought her back
to her own people.

The song was sung,
the poet's tale was told.
Merriment arose again,
a bright sound from the benches.
Cup bearers poured out wine from wondrous flagons.

Queen Wealtheow speaks

Then Wealtheow came forth again
gliding under her golden circlet
to where the good pair, Hrothgar and his nephew Hrothulf, sat.
Their friendship was still strong and true to one another.
Likewise the spokesman Unferth settled
at the feet of the Scylding lord. Everyone trusted
his spirit, considered him courageous, even though
he had not treated his kinsmen honorably
at swordplay. The lady of the Scyldings spoke:
"Drink this full cup, my noble lord
and treasure-giver! Be merry
my dear gold-friend, and speak gracious words
to the Geats, like a man should do!
Be generous with them, remembering the many gifts
you own, from far and near.

"I hear that you would take this man
as your own son. Heorot, this bright hall of rings
has now been cleansed. Make use of your many gifts
while you still can, before you leave your land
and people to your kinsmen, and go forth
to meet your fate.

"I know in my heart that gracious Hrothulf here
will protect these young warriors with honor
if you, friend of the Scyldings,
should let go of this world before him.
I'm sure he will repay our sons with kindness
remembering the benefits that we bestowed
upon him in his youth, to his delight and honor."

She turned now to the bench
where her children, Hrethric and Hrothmund,
and all the sons of warriors sat together.
There too was Beowulf, hero of the Geats,
seated between the two brothers.

A brimming cup was brought to Beowulf.
Friendship was offered him in words
and woven gold was graciously bestowed—
two arm-bands, chain-mail, rings,
and the greatest golden collar
that I have ever heard of on this earth.

I have never heard of any better
hoard-treasure for a hero under heaven
since Hama bore away the Brosing's necklace,
the jewels in their precious setting,
to the bright castle. He escaped the cunning plots
of Eormenric, and chose an eternal reward.

The collar's future fate

Hygelac the Geat, Swerting's nephew, would take
that necklace with him on his final voyage,
defended that treasure beneath his banner,
guarding the spoils of battle. Fate seized him then,
when, out of arrogance, he went looking for a fight

with the Frisians. The powerful prince
had worn that treasure with its precious stones
over the ocean's brimming cup,
only to end up crumpled beneath his shield.

His life, his chain mail and the necklace
fell into Frisian hands—
lesser warriors robbed the slaughtered
after the scythe of battle mowed them down.
The Geats gained nothing but a field of corpses.

Wealtheow's blessing

Placing the golden collar on Beowulf's neck,
Wealtheow spoke to the company of warriors:

"Enjoy this ring, beloved Beowulf.
Wear it in good health, young man,
and make good use of this mail shirt
from the people's treasure. May you thrive and prosper,
show your strength, and be a gentle teacher
to these boys. For this, I will always remember
and reward you. You have conducted yourself
so that men will admire you forever
as far and wide as the sea,
dwelling place of the wind, rings its cliffs.

"Be happy as long as you live, dear prince!
I have done right by you in giving treasure—
be gracious to my sons, most blessed man.
Here, all men are true to one another,
courteous and loyal to their lord.
The thanes are united, the people prepared.
The warriors who drink here do as I bid them to."

She returned to her seat.
The choicest of feasts was set before them.
They drank their wine, little suspecting their fate,
the grim lot that befell so many men
when evening fell, and Hrothgar sought
his place of rest.

Episode Two

GRENDEL'S MOTHER

Grendel's mother comes to Heorot

Countless men guarded the hall
the way they used to do,
setting the benches aside
and scattering beds and pillows.
One of those beer-drinkers
curled up on the floor
was about to meet his fate.

At their heads they placed their shining shields,
on the bench beside them, towering battle helms,
ringed corselets and mighty wooden spears.
It was their habit, whether at home or in the field
to always be ready to fight
whenever their ruler might need them.
It was a good troop.

They sank into sleep. One would pay dearly
for his evening's rest, as so often happened
when Grendel ruled the golden hall,
committing crimes until his end had come,
paying for his sins with death.

But soon it was clear to everyone
that his avenger lived.
Grendel's mother, a monster-woman
was gnawed by her war-grief
long after the battle.

The water-terror
had lived in the coldest currents
ever since Cain had killed his only brother,
his closest kin. He went forth blood-stained,

marked by murder. Fleeing the joys of men
he wandered the wilderness.

From him fate awakened
all kinds of demons—Grendel was one,
a savage outcast filled with hate
who found one man awake in Heorot,
awaiting his attack.

That man had been in the monster's grip
but he remembered his mighty strength, the ample gift
which God had given him, trusted himself
to the Lord for favor, comfort and support.
This was how he overcame the fiend, humbled
that spirit from Hell. Mankind's enemy fled,
bereft of joy, to find his deathbed.

But Grendel's mother, in a gallows mood
was eager to pay a grieving visit
to avenge her son.
The Ring-Danes were sleeping
scattered about the hall
when she came to Heorot.
Things quickly took a turn for the worse
when Grendel's mother got in.

The terror was only less
by as much as a woman warrior's strength
would be, compared to a weaponed man
when the sword's tough edge,
blood-stained and hammer-forged
bites into the boar-crest helmet guard.

The men in the hall grabbed hard-edged swords
from the benches. Many had wide shields
in their grip. But nobody thought
about helmets or mail shirts
when seized with a sudden terror.

Found out, she was now in a hurry to flee,
get away with her life. Quickly she grabbed
one princely man, clutched him tight in her grasp
and fled back to the fens.

He had been Hrothgar's dearest companion
between the two seas, a mighty shield-man,
a glorious hero she murdered in his sleep.

Beowulf was not in the hall.
Another place had been granted the famous Geat
after the treasure-giving.

Heorot was in an uproar.
Grendel's mother had taken the bloody hand
she knew so well.
Sorrow sprang up again—
it was no happy exchange
when both sides had to pay
with a loved one's life.

Hrothgar breaks the news to Beowulf

Then the wise old king,
the gray warrior, was filled with grief
when he learned that his dearest thane
was dead. Beowulf was summoned
to his chamber, the man blessed with victory.
At daybreak he came with his noble troop
where the wise man waited, wondering,
after this terrible news, if the Lord
would ever change his luck.

The hall-wood resounded
as the hero and his hand-picked soldiers
walked across the floor. He addressed
the lord of the Ingwines, asking Hrothgar
whether he had passed a pleasant night.

"Don't speak to me of pleasure!"
Hrothgar, helm of the Scyldings, cried.
"Sorrow has struck the Danish nation
once again. Aeschere is dead—
Yrmenlaf's older brother, my confidant and counselor.
We stood shoulder to shoulder in battle
warding off blows to our helms
as troops clashed and boar-crests collided.
Every man should be as Aeschere was.

"He was killed in Heorot, at the hand
of some restless, murderous demon.
I'm not sure where she escaped to,
proud of his corpse and glad to get her fill.

"She was avenging the fight
where you killed Grendel by the force
of your hard grip the other night,
because he had wasted and destroyed
my people far too long. He fell in battle,
his life the payment for his guilt. And now
another has come, a mighty man-killer
to avenge her kinsman.

"She has taken the feud too far,
it will seem to many thanes,
whose spirits grieve now for their treasure-giver.
A hard blow to the heart, now that the hand
which granted every wish lies powerless.

The haunted mere

"I hear tell from my counselors
who live in that part of the country
that they have seen two such giants
wandering the wasteland, alien spirits
who ruled the moors.

"One, as far as they could see,
was in the likeness of a woman.
The other wretched being
trod the tracks of exile
in the form of a man, but bigger
than any other. In days of yore
the country folk called him Grendel.
No one knew his father, nor what other
dark spirits he may have begot.

"They dwelt in wolf caves
in that secret land, wind-blown cliffs,
treacherous fen-paths where the mountain streams
disappear beneath the crags, deep under ground.

"Not far from here, as miles are measured,
you'll find the mere.
Over it hang frosted trees,
firm-rooted woods overshadowing the lake.
There, every night a fearful wonder
can be seen—fire rising from the water.
No living man, however old,
has ever seen the bottom.

"The strong-antlered hart
who leaps across the heath
pursued far afield by the hounds
may seek those woods—
but he'd sooner lay down his life
on that shore than save his skin
by jumping into the water.
That is no good place!

"When the wind stirs bad weather
surging waves are churned up there,
clawing their way to the clouds
till the sky turns dark and gloomy
and the heavens weep.

"Once again, only you can advise me.
You have not yet seen the perilous place
where you might find that sinful creature.
Seek it if you dare!
I will reward you for this fight
with treasure, as I did before—
ancient heirlooms, torcs of twisted gold—
if you come back alive."

Beowulf encourages Hrothgar. They set out.

Beowulf, the son of Ecgtheow, spoke:
"Do not sorrow, man of wisdom!
It is always better to avenge a friend
than to mourn too much.
An end to this worldly life
comes for us all. Let him who can
win fame before his death—

that is the best thing for a man
when life has left him.

"Arise, defender of the kingdom!
Let's go quickly now
and look at the track that Grendel's kin has left.
I promise you this: she cannot hide,
not in the earth's embrace, nor in the forest depths,
nor at the bottom of the sea, go where she will!
Be strong today in facing every woe—
I expect no less from you!"

The old man jumped up
and gave thanks to God
for the words that man had spoken.
Then Hrothgar's horse with its braided mane
was bridled, and the wise prince
rode forth in all his splendor
accompanied by warriors bearing shields.

Her track through the woods
could be seen by all. The trail headed
straight for the murky moors
where she had borne, bereft of soul,
the best of all the thanes
who ruled their homes with Hrothgar.

The noble troop rode narrow paths
over steep stone cliffs, unknown trails
across precipitous ridges pocked
with water-monsters' dens. A few scouts,
men of experience, showed the way.

The mere

Suddenly they came across mountain trees
leaning out over large gray stones, a gloomy wood.
The water that stood underneath
was bubbling with blood.

The Danes and their friends were stricken to the soul,
every last thane, when they discovered
sitting on a cliff by the water side
the head of Aeschere.

The men watched the water boiling up
with hot blood and gore.
A horn rang out time and again
its fierce battle cry.
They braced themselves.

In the water they saw serpents writhing,
strange sea-demons sounding the depths.
Water monsters lay on the rocky slopes
who often, at morning, made their sorry way
to the sail-roads: snakes and such wild beasts.
They slithered off, bitter and angry,
when they heard the war-horn singing
its bright song.

A Geat soldier with his bow
split one of the water-thrashers
from its life; its swimming weaker
as death's grip grew stronger,
a hard war-arrow in its guts.
Quickly it was attacked, hard pressed
with the barbed heads of boar spears
and dragged out onto the rocky slope,
that wondrous roamer of the waves.
The men gazed at their terrible guest.

Beowulf prepares himself. Unferth offers Hrunting.

Beowulf girded himself in war gear,
not the least bit worried for his life.
His mail-shirt, broad, hand-woven,
artfully adorned, would test those depths.
It knew how to protect his house of bones
so the crush of battle, an angry enemy's grip
could not reach his heart nor harm his life.

A shining helmet stood guard upon his head
which would soon be stirring the depths of the mere,
seeking out the surging waters. Crusted with jewels,
it was circled by a princely band, wondrously worked
in days of old by the weapon smith, set all about
with images of boars, so that ever after
no brand nor blade could bite it.

Not the smallest support to his strength
was the hafted sword that Hrothgar's spokesman Unferth
gave him now in his hour of need.
Its name was Hrunting. The greatest of heirlooms,
its edge was iron, etched with acid
and hardened in the blood of battle.
It had never failed any man in a fight
who grasped it with his hand and dared to go
on a dangerous foray against an enemy fort.
This was not the first time
it was called on to perform a work of courage.

Unferth, Ecglaf's strong and crafty son
was certainly not thinking now
of the words he had spoken when drunk with wine
as he handed over the sword to the better swordsman.
He himself did not dare
to risk his life beneath the troubled waters,
to bear himself heroically—there he gave up glory
and fame for valor.

Last words to Hrothgar

It was not so with the other man,
now that he had girded himself for battle.
Beowulf, the son of Ecgtheow, spoke:
"Bear in mind, great son of Healfdane,
wise ruler and gold-friend of men,
now that I am ready to set forth,
remember the words that we two spoke—
if, helping you in your hardship
I should lose my life, when I departed
you would act as a father would.

"Be a protector to my thanes.
Hold them in your hands,
my close companions, if battle takes me.
And the treasures you've given me,
send them, dear Hrothgar, to Hygelac.
Then the lord of the Geats, son of Hrethel,
gazing upon the gold and jewels, will realize
I found a ring-giver both good and generous
and enjoyed it while I could.

"And please give to Unferth
the ancient treasure I inherited—
this wave-sword, worked in wondrous patterns.
Let that famous man have its hard-edged blade.
With Hrunting I will win my fame
or death will take me!"

Into the mere

After these words the Storm-Geats' lord
plunged bravely ahead, without waiting for an answer.
The surging waters embraced the warrior.
It took a good part of the day
to find the bottom. Before long
the one who had ruled these waters
half a hundred years—grim, greedy
and eager for battle—realized
that a man from up above
had found that alien creature's home.

She groped her way towards him,
grabbing the man in her terrible claws.
But still no harm came to his body—
ring mail protected him all around.
She could not pierce his war-coat,
his locked limb-shirt, with her hateful fingers.

The sea-wolf bore him to the bottom,
dragged the ring-lord down to her den.
He couldn't struggle free to wield his weapons,
no matter how brave he might be.
Strange creatures tormented him: sea-beasts

with sharp battle-tusks attacked his armor,
monsters harried and pursued him.

He soon found himself
in some sort of enemy hall
where no water could touch him:
the hall's roof prevented any harm
from the flood's sudden grip.
He could see the brilliant gleam
of a fire's light.

The fight with Grendel's mother

Then he saw the damned monster of the deep,
the mighty mere-wife. He swung
his battle sword in a powerful rush—
his hand held nothing back,
so that the ring-hilted sword
came down upon her head
singing its terrible war-song.

But her guest soon found out
that his battle-flame would not bite her
nor harm her life in the least—its edge
had failed him in his time of need.
It had stood up to so many
meetings of hands, sheared so many helmets
and mail-shirts of the doomed.
This was the first time that the priceless treasure
had fallen short of its fame.

Hygelac's kinsman did not hesitate—
his mind was set on glory
and his courage never faltered.
The angry warrior threw away
the splendid treasure sword.
Its hard edge of steel hit the ground.
Instead, he trusted to his strength,
the powerful grip of his hand.
This is what a man should do—
abandon all care about his life
when he wants to win lasting fame in battle.

But she quickly paid him back
with her own fierce grip,
threw herself against him
so that the strongest man alive,
the champion in battle,
stumbled and fell to the ground.

Sitting on top of her hall-guest,
she drew her broad and bright-edged dagger—
the time had come to avenge her child,
her only son.

Across his chest lay a net of woven mail.
It saved him, forbidding entry to point and edge.
He would have lost his life deep underground,
the son of Ecgtheow, champion of the Geats,
if his armor, his hard war-shirt, had not helped him—
and holy God as well, wise Lord and Heaven's Ruler,
who would rightly and easily decide the victory
once Beowulf got back on his feet again.

Among the war-gear there he saw
a gigantic ancient sword,
tough-edged and victory-blessed,
a choice weapon, glory of warriors.
But it was bigger than any other man
could bear into battle,
a great and splendid work of giants.

The Scylding's champion grabbed the hilt.
Fierce and savage, reckless of his life
he swung the sword, striking with such fury
that the blade bit into her neck
and broke the bone-rings.
The sword cut clean
through her doomed house of flesh.
She crumpled to the floor.
The blade was dripping blood,
the man rejoicing in his work.

Deeper into the den

A gleam flashed out, a glow within
as when the light of heaven's candle
is shining bright. He looked around the cave
and carefully advanced along the wall,
holding the hilt of his weapon tight.
Its edge would not prove useless
to Hygelac's thane.

Angry and determined, he intended
to pay Grendel back, and soon,
for his many attacks upon the Danish people.
There had been many more than the one
where he slew Hrothgar's thanes in their sleep,
devouring fifteen of the sleeping Danes
and carrying off as many more,
his horrible spoils of battle.

The fierce champion handed him
his reward for that—so much so
that now he saw Grendel
in his final resting place,
lifeless and weary of war,
dead from his battle wound at Heorot.

The corpse sprang open
suffering a sword-stroke after death
a hard blow, as Beowulf
cut the head clean from its body.

The Danes lose hope

Soon the wise counselors
who gazed with Hrothgar upon the water
saw the waves begin to brim with blood.
The grizzled old men were all agreed—
the hero would not be coming back victorious
to their great king. It looked to most
like the sea-wolf had slaughtered him.

When the ninth hour came
The brave Scyldings abandoned the headland.
The gold-friend of the people went back home.

Their guests, the Geats, sat down
and stared at the water, sick at heart.
They still hoped, but no longer expected
to see their friend and lord again.

Strange magic

Meanwhile, the sword in Beowulf's hand
began to melt from the monster's blood,
that battle-sweat,
like some great icicle of war.
It was a wonder, as it all dissolved
just as the ice does when our Father,
ruler of the times and seasons,
loosens and unbinds the water's chains,
the fetters of frost.
He is the true Creator.

The lord of the Weather-Geats
took nothing more from that place,
although he saw treasures all around him,
than that head and the jeweled hilt.
The sword had already melted away,
its inlaid blade burnt up—the blood
of the poisonous demons who died there
had been so hot.

Soon he was swimming again.
Having seen his enemies fall in battle
he plunged upward through the water.
The wide dwelling-place of the waves
was completely cleansed since that strange spirit
let go of her life's days in this fleeting world.

Joy among the Geats

And so the defender of the seamen
came swimming, stouthearted, at last to land.
He rejoiced in the heavy sea-plunder
he carried with him. A crowd of noble thanes
gathered about him, thanking God,
rejoicing to see their lord again, safe and sound.

Helmet and mail shirt they quickly untied
from the rugged warrior. The water calmed down,
dyed, beneath the clouds, with deadly blood.

Glad at heart, they set forth on the footpaths,
pacing out the familiar country ways. Brave as kings,
the men bore Grendel's head from the water-cliff.
This was a hard job for them:
it was the work of four stout men
to bear it on a spear to the golden hall.

Before long, fourteen brave and battle-eager Geats
arrived at the hall, their high-spirited leader among them.
Treading the meadows of the clearing, the lord of thanes
now entered Heorot. Daring in deeds,
exalted in glory, he greeted Hrothgar.

The head of Grendel was carried by the hair
onto the hall floor where the men were drinking
and brought before the nobles, the queen among them.
All gazed at the terrible and wondrous sight.

Beowulf tells of his battle in the mere

Beowulf, the son of Ecgtheow, spoke:
"Behold this sea-gift, son of Healfdane,
lord of the Scyldings, this token of victory
we bring here joyfully for you to see.
It was no easy matter, to survive
that war under water, the difficult work
I undertook. I would have lost the battle
right away, had God not shielded me.
Nor could I accomplish anything at all
with Hrunting, worthy as that weapon was.

"But the Ruler of mankind, who often helps
the friendless man, granted I should see
hanging upon the wall an ancient sword,
huge and glittering. I drew that weapon.
As soon as I had the chance, I struck
and slew the guardian of the house.

"Then the wave-patterned blade burned up
from the blood that sprang forth,
steaming battle-sweat. I took the hilt
from the enemy, having avenged their crimes,
the deadly slaughter they brought the Danes,
as was fitting and proper.

"And now I promise you can sleep in Heorot
without sorrow amid your company of men,
all your thanes, young and old, without dreading
manslaughter from that side, as you did before."

Hrothgar examines the wondrous hilt

Then the golden hilt, the work of giants long ago
was placed in the old warrior's hand,
that gray-haired battle-chief. After the devils' downfall
that work of wondrous smiths now passed
into possession of the Danish lord.

Once that angry heart, God's enemy,
murder-guilty along with his mother,
gave up this world, the hilt had come
into the keeping of the world's best king
between the two seas, who ruled
the Danish realm and gave out treasure.

Hrothgar, about to speak, gazed at the hilt.
Engraved on that heirloom
was the origin of that ancient strife
when the Flood struck the race of giants.
A people alien to the eternal Lord,
they had acted outrageously.
The Ruler of the world had sealed their fate,
the rushing waters their last reward.

On the shining gold sword-guard,
correctly written in runic letters, was the name
of the one the sword had been made for,
the choicest of iron blades, with its twisted hilt
and dragon decoration.

For Beowulf, praise—

Then the wise son of Healfdane spoke
and all fell silent:

"One who has done truth and right
for his people, an old ruler
who remembers long ago,
can truly say
that this man was born better!

"My dear friend Beowulf,
your fame is established across the wide ways,
among all the nations and peoples.
You have governed your might and power
with wisdom of heart and mind.
I shall keep those vows of friendship
that we spoke before.
Long will you be a comfort to your people,
a help to your warriors.

—and a warning

"Heremod was not like that
to the sons of Ecgwela, the Honor-Scyldings.
He grew up to accomplish, not their desires,
but the death and slaughter of the Danish people.
In his rages, he cut down his table companions,
those who stood shoulder to shoulder beside him,
until that great lord ended up alone,
cut off from the happiness of men.

"Mighty God had given him the joys of strength,
advanced him in power above all others.
But his spirit, the heart in his chest
grew more and more thirsty for blood.
He never gave rings to the Danes
to win praise and glory. Joyless he lived,
suffering from the long affliction
that he caused his people.

"Learn from that—
grasp the meaning
of manly virtue and generosity!
Old in winters, I tell this tale
for your sake, Beowulf.

The dangers of kingship

"It is a wonder to tell
how mighty God, from his great spirit
gives mankind wisdom, property and power.
He rules over all. Sometimes,
out of love, he gives free play
to the spirit of a noble man,
gives him earthly joy in his own country,
strong towns of men to hold,
deals out to him as his domain
such great realms, wide reaches,
that, lacking wisdom, a man cannot imagine
all this ever coming to an end.

"His life is a feast. He never dwells
upon old age or illness, nor does resentment
rankle in his breast. No quarrels of any kind
bare the sword's hateful edge. The world
revolves around his pleasure.
He knows nothing worse, until pride
and overconfidence grow rank within
and the guard keeping watch on his soul
goes to sleep.

"That sleep is too sound,
surrounded by troubles. His bane
is all too close, with his bow
and arrows of evil. Then he is struck
in the heart, beneath his helmet
by the bitter shafts—he has no defense
against the strange and dark commands
of the cursed demon.

"All that he has long enjoyed
now seems to him too little. He grows
vicious and greedy. He gives no jeweled rings
for the sake of glory. He forgets
about the life to come, ignores
the fame and honor that God gave him.

"When the final runes are written,
the body, this temporary shelter, fails him.
He falls to fate, and another takes his place
who gives out treasure without grieving,
not afraid to share his noble heirlooms.

An old king's advice

"Defend yourself against those attacks,
dear Beowulf, best of men,
and choose the better, the eternal counsel.
Pay no heed to pride, great champion!

"Now you are blessed with strength a little while.
Too soon, illness or a blade's edge
will cut off your power—or the fire's grasp
or the flood's waves, the sword's grip
the spear's flight, or terrible old age.
The light of your eyes
will dim and at last burn out
and sudden death will overcome you, warrior.

"Just so, I have ruled the Ring-Danes under heaven
for half a hundred years, protected them in war
from the ashwood shafts and edges
of many nations on this middle earth,
until at last, beneath the sky's domain
I counted no one as my enemy.

"But look now—in my own home
things changed for the worse. Grief
followed joy after Grendel came,
my invader and life-enemy. That strife
caused endless turmoil, overwhelming sorrow.
Now let the Creator be thanked,

the eternal Lord, that I have lived,
after such long struggle,
to gaze at that bloody head with my own eyes!

"Go to your seat now, and enjoy the feast,
having won glory in battle. Many treasures
shall pass between us when the morning comes."

A well-earned rest

The Geat hero, glad at heart,
quickly sought out his seat
as the wise king asked him.
Then once again the feast was set out
for the valiant warriors sitting in the hall.

The helm of night descended, darkening
over the company. The troop all arose.
The gray-haired old man of the Scyldings
wished to seek his bed. In the Geat hero too,
that brave shield-bearer, there suddenly welled up
a measureless longing for rest.

A hall-thane led him forth,
the man come from afar,
and with courtesy attended to such needs
as, in those days, a noble thane
and seafaring warrior might have.

The big-hearted man
was at rest in the towering hall
gabled and inlaid with gold
until at last the black raven
with a blithe spirit boded heaven's joy.

Farewells and pledges of friendship

Then brightness came quickly,
banishing the shadows.
The warriors made haste, eager
to be setting sail for home again.
The guest, filled with excitement, was ready
to seek out his ship for a distant voyage.

Then the hardy man had them bring Hrunting
to Unferth, Ecglaf's son, told him
to take the sword, that lovely steel,
and thanked him for the loan.
He reckoned it a good friend
in a fight, a war-crafty weapon,
had not a word to say against its edge—
his was a generous spirit.

The men had their gear all ready to depart.
Their noble prince, so honored by the Danes,
now approached the high throne.
The brave warrior gave greetings to Hrothgar.
Beowulf, the son of Ecgtheow, spoke:

"We seafarers, come from afar, now wish to say
that we are eager to seek out Hygelac.
We have been most agreeably entertained.
You have done well by us.
If I can do anything on earth
in the way of war-work
that will better earn your love
I will not hesitate to do it.

"If I find out, far over the floodways,
that your neighbors are oppressing you with terror
as your enemies have done before,
I will bring a thousand thanes,
heroes to your help.

"I know that Hygelac lord of the Geats,
our people's protector, young though he may be,
will back me up with word and work
so I can honor you,
carry a spear shaft to your aid,
support you with all my strength
when you have need of men.

"And if the king's son Hrethric
should come to the court of the Geats
he will find many a friend there.
Distant countries are best visited
by a man who's worth something himself."

Hrothgar's prophetic farewell

Hrothgar spoke in reply:
"The words you have spoken were placed in your heart
by the all-knowing Lord.
Never have I heard anyone so young
speak with such distinction.
You are not only great in strength
but wise in word and spirit!

"I should think, if grim war's spear,
disease or steel should bear off Hrethel's son,
your lord and the people's protector
while you are still alive, the Geats
could make no better choice for king,
guardian of the heroes' hoard, if you consent
to rule the kingdom of your kin.

"Your spirit pleases me more
the longer I know you, dear Beowulf.
Thanks to you, the Danes and Geats
shall be as brothers—attacks and injuries
that each endured before shall cease.

"As long as I rule this broad realm
we shall trade treasures instead.
Many more will bring greetings
over the gannet's bath,
ringed prows on the high seas
bearing gifts and tokens of our love.

"I know that our people
stand fast with their friends
and firm against their foes—
in every way blameless,
as in days of old."

The moment of parting

Healfdane's kinsman, protector of noble men
gave Beowulf twelve more treasures in that hall,
bade him, with those gifts

seek out his beloved land in safety
and come back soon again.

Then the good king of the Scyldings
clasped the neck of the best of thanes
and kissed him. Tears ran
down the cheeks of that grizzled old man.

Of the two fates, the wise elder
thought one more likely—
these two brave spirits
would never meet again.

So dear was this man to him, he could not bear
the waves of feeling welling in his breast.
Deep in his heart, bound fast by thought,
secret longing burned within his blood.

Beowulf turned and walked away,
the gold-bedecked warrior treading the grass,
rejoicing in his treasure. His ship,
riding at anchor, awaited its master.

The coast guard sings a different tune

On the march, they all praised Hrothgar's generosity.
Here was a king who was truly faultless—
until old age, the bane of so many,
had taken the joy of his strength away.
In high spirits, the crowd of young men
went down to the water wearing their ring-nets,
locked protectors of life and limb.

The coast guard saw them coming back,
as he had seen them come to land before.
This time there would be no challenge from the cliff—
rather, he rode out to greet them
saying that the Weather-Geats would welcome
these bright-clad warriors headed for their ship.

The broad sea vessel rested on the sand.
They loaded the curved prow with war gear,
horses and treasure. The mast towered high
above Hrothgar's hoard. Beowulf gave the guard

a gold-inlaid sword, so that ever after
he would be more honored at the mead bench
as the owner of that treasured heirloom.

Episode Three

THE DRAGON

The voyage home

They shoved off in the ship,
stirring the deep waters,
leaving the Danish land behind.
The sail, a great sea cloak,
was fastened to the mast.
The sea-wood groaned and creaked.

No contrary winds impeded their journey.
The foamy-necked craft floated over the waves
the strong prow crossing the currents
until they could see the well-known cliffs
of Geatland, and driven by the wind
the keel was thrust up on the beach.

Quickly the harbor guard, alert and ready
came down to the shore. For a long time now
he had eagerly gazed far out to sea
on watch for these well-loved men.

He moored the broad-bosomed ship in sand
making it fast with anchor ropes
lest the crash of waves should carry off
that handsome wood.

Beowulf ordered them to bear away
the princely treasure, jeweled and filigreed with gold.
Nor did they have far to seek
for their own treasure-giver: Hygelac Hrethling
and his comrades lived close by the seawall.
The hall building was high and splendid,
the king renowned for valor.

Queen Hygd was very young
but she excelled in wisdom.
Though the daughter of Haereth
had not passed many winters in the hall-fort
she was never mean or stingy
in giving gifts of treasure to the Geats.

Modthryth compared to Hygd

Modthryth, on the other hand,
once a proud queen of that people,
had committed terrible crimes.
None of the hall companions but her lord
dared look on her face in the light of day.
Whoever did knew what his fate would be:
his hands would be twisted in murderous thongs,
then quickly the inlaid sword would be called for
to clear up the matter with slaughter.

That was not a queenly custom,
nor fitting for a lady—
for a woman, a weaver of peace,
however peerless her beauty,
to take the lives of beloved men
over pretended insults.

Hemming's kinsman Offa
soon put a stop to that.
Over their ale, men tell another story—
how the bane of her people was less inclined to crime
after she was given, adorned with gold
to that young champion of high nobility,
seeking out, on her father's advice,
the court of Offa over the glimmering sea.

Ever after, she was famed for goodness
on her throne, enjoyed and did well with
the days she was given, harboring a noble love
for that lord of heroes who, I've heard,
was the best man between the two seas.

For Offa, that spear-keen man,
was widely honored both for generosity
and warfare. He ruled his kingdom wisely.
From him sprang Eomer, help of heroes,
Hemming's kin and Garmund's grandson,
strong and skillful in battle.

Welcome in the hall of Hygelac

The sturdy warrior strode along the sand
treading the wide shore with his handpicked men.
The candle of the world shone bright,
its light streaming eagerly from the south.
Having survived their journey
they hurried toward the fortress
where they heard that their young king,
the slayer of Ongentheow, was giving out rings.

Hygelac was quickly told of Beowulf's return—
his shield-companion, defender of warriors,
had come home from his sword-play unscathed.
The king ordered room in the court quickly cleared
for the guests coming in.

The man who had come through such struggles
loyally greeted his lord
with formal yet heartfelt words
then sat down beside him
as kinsman with kinsman.

Haereth's daughter took care of her people,
passing the mead cups around the hall,
placing a flagon in each man's hand.

His curiosity about to burst,
Hygelac, with great courtesy
began to question his hall companion
about the Sea Geat's journey.

"How did things go on your voyage,
dear Beowulf, when you suddenly decided
to seek out struggle far away
across the salt water, a fight at Heorot?
Did you help Hrothgar somewhat,
that great lord with his well-known troubles?

"I went through worries and waves of sorrow—
I had no confidence in that undertaking.
Time and again I asked you
not to go near that murderous demon
but let the South-Danes settle their own struggle
against Grendel. I give thanks to God
that I can see you once more safe and sound."

Beowulf begins his story

Beowulf, the son of Ecgtheow, spoke:
"It's no secret, lord Hygelac,
but known to many men, that meeting
between me and Grendel—
the one who caused the Victory-Scyldings
so many sorrows, made their life a misery.

"I avenged all that.
None of Grendel's kin on earth—
whoever lives longest, steeped in sin,
of that hateful race—needs to boast
of our clash in the dark.

"First I went straight to the ring-hall
and gave greetings to Hrothgar.
When the great kinsman of Healfdane
heard what was on my mind
he quickly gave me a seat
next to his own sons.

"The company was filled with joy—
never in my life, under heaven's roof
have I seen hall guests
who enjoyed their mead so much.

"From time to time the great queen,
pledge of peace between nations,
moved about the hall
encouraging the young men,
giving out twisted rings of gold
before she at last took her seat.

"Now and again Hrothgar's daughter
brought flagons of ale for the troops.
I heard men call her Freaware
as she offered the studded cup.

"Young and gold-adorned, she has been promised
to the gracious son of Froda.
The lord and shepherd of the Scyldings
considers it good counsel
to settle their many blood feuds with this woman.
But the spear of slaughter seldom rests for long
after a king has fallen,
no matter how worthy the bride!

How feuds flare up. Dire predictions
for the marriage with Ingeld, son of Froda.

"For it may not please the son of Froda,
lord of the Heathobards, nor his retainers
to see the noble youths of Denmark
walk into their hall with that woman
to be splendidly entertained.

"On the Danes they see glittering
their own ancestors' heirlooms,
hard and ring-patterned, the Heathobards' treasures,
the weapons they had wielded while they could,
before they sacrificed in shield-play
their dear companions and their very lives.

"Spying those treasures over his beer,
a grim old spearman, who remembers
all that slaughter, in his bitterness begins
to test the temper, try the hidden heart
of some young champion,
goading him to fight. He says:

"'Might you, my young friend, recognize
that sword your father bore into battle
the last time that he ever wore a helmet—
the beloved blade he held
when the Danes, these brave Scyldings,
struck him down?
They ruled that slaughter-ground
after Withergild lay dead
and all of our heroes had fallen.

"'Now the son of one of his killers
walks the floor of our hall
flaunting his fancy trappings,
boasting about that murder
and bearing the precious treasure
that should by right be yours.'"

"With painful words he keeps on goading
at every opportunity, until at last
the woman's thane lies stained with blood,
put to sleep by the sword's bite, sacrificed
for his father's deeds.
The other man, knowing the lay of the land,
escapes with his life.

"Then, on both sides, sword oaths are broken.
A murderous hatred wells up within Ingeld
and, overwhelmed by care and sorrow,
his love for his wife grows cool.

"So I do not believe the Heathobards
will be loyal, their peace with the Danes
without deceit, their friendship fast.

Meanwhile, back at Heorot…

"But now let me get back to Grendel
so you can hear, treasure-giver,
how that hand-to-hand combat came out.

"After the jewel of heaven
had gone gliding over the earth,
that angry spirit, evil thing of evening,
came looking where we, so far safe,
kept watch in the hall.

"Handscioh was the first
to be taken in the attack,
doomed by that deadly evil.
Grendel tore into that champion with his teeth,
swallowed the body of that beloved man.

"The bloody-toothed killer was not yet ready
to leave the gold-hall empty-handed.
He had murder on his mind.
Made bold by his strength,
he decided to give me a try
and made an eager grab.

"A big, strange bag
hung from his hand,
held fast by cunning clasps—
it was cleverly made by the devil's craft
out of a dragon's skin.
The bold thief wanted to put me inside it
along with many other innocent men.
But it was not to be that night
as soon as I stood upright in my anger.

"It would take too long to tell
the way I repaid that man-killer for his crimes
but my work there brought honor to your people.
He escaped to enjoy his life a little while
but his right hand stayed behind in Heorot
when he plunged in grief to the bottom of the mere.

King Hrothgar sings

"When morning came and we sat down to the feast
the friend of the Scyldings rewarded me
for that deadly fight with gifts of gold and treasure.

"There was song and story. An ancient Scylding
steeped in knowledge, told of long ago.
At times he brought joy from the harp,
playing upon the pleasant wood. At times
he chanted a song both sad and true.

"At times the great-hearted king himself
would rightly recite a marvelous tale.
Then again the old warrior, bound by age,
would mourn for his youth and battle-strength.
Wise in winters, his heart welled up within him
as he remembered so much. And so
we took our pleasures all day long
until another night had come to men.

Grendel's mother and her den

"Then suddenly Grendel's mother came,
filled with sorrow,
eager to avenge her grief.
Death had taken her son
in his feud with the Weders.

"That unholy woman avenged her son,
boldly killing a man. There lay Aeschere,
the wise old counselor, his spirit fleeing.
Nor could the death-weary Danes
burn his body, lift the beloved man
onto his funeral pyre. His corpse
was borne away in the fiend's embrace
beneath the mountain stream.

"For Hrothgar, that grief was the bitterest yet.
Fiercely, passionately he implored me,
upon your life, to throw myself into that water,
do a noble deed, to risk my life for glory.
He promised to reward me well.

"Under the surging water, as is widely known,
I found the terrible guardian of the deep.
For a while we engaged in hand-to-hand combat.
Then the water was welling with blood—

I cut off the head of Grendel's mother
With a mighty edge. It wasn't easy
escaping with my life, but my time
had not yet come.

Generous gifts of treasure

"Healfdane's kinsman, defender of nobles,
gave me great treasures afterwards.
The king followed good custom.
I did not lose out, by any means,
on the rewards due to valor:
the son of Healfdane gave me any treasure
I would choose. And now, king of men,
I present them to you. To you,
as always, I owe every joy.
I have few close kinsmen,
Hygelac, except for you."

He ordered them to bring in the boar's head banner,
the high battle helmet, the gray coat of mail,
and the terrible war-sword. Then he made this speech:

"Hrothgar, prince among the wise,
gave me this battle gear
and asked me to say a few words about it.
He told me king Heorogar, the Scylding lord,
had owned it a long time, but even so
never gave this chest protector to his son,
loyal and brave as Heoroweard had been. Enjoy it well!"

I've heard that, on the heels of those precious ornaments,
four well-matched apple-fallow horses quickly followed.
He gave Hygelac the horses and the treasure.

This is how kinsmen should act,
not weaving cunning snares for one another,
contriving death with secret craft
for their closest companions.
To Hygelac the hard warrior
his nephew was staunchly loyal,
each mindful of the welfare of the other.

I heard he gave queen Hygd the golden necklace,
wondrously worked, that Wealtheow had given him,
along with three horses, graceful and bright-saddled.
After the ring-giving, that treasure adorned her breast.

This is how Beowulf bore himself,
the son of Ecgtheow, famed in battle,
acting with honor and generosity.
He never drunkenly struck his hearth companions.
His was not an angry spirit. No,
that valiant warrior, strongest of all mankind,
knew how to guard the ample gifts
that God had given him.

For a long time he had been scorned.
The sons of the Geats gave him little honor
on the mead bench, considered him slack
and slothful, a lazy prince. But now
it had all turned around—every trouble
was gone for the man now blessed with glory.

The courageous king, protector of nobles,
ordered them to bring in Hrethel's heirloom.
Resplendent in gold, the Geats possessed
no finer treasure sword.
He laid it in Beowulf's lap,
and then bestowed on him seven thousand
hides of land, a hall and a princely throne.
Both had inherited land in the kingdom,
with ancestral rights, but the man of higher rank
ruled the broadest realm.

Beowulf becomes king. An ancient evil is awakened.

In later days it came about
through the fortunes of war that Hygelac fell
and Heardred his son was also slain
by swords behind the shield wall.
The War-Scilfings, hard fighters
sought out Hereric's nephew, attacked him fiercely
in the midst of his warriors.

Then the broad kingdom
passed into Beowulf's hands.
He ruled it well for fifty winters,
a wise old king and guardian of his land

…until a dragon
began to rule the dark nights.
It guarded a treasure hoard on the upland heath
in a high stone barrow. Underneath lay a path
unknown to men.

Some unknown passer-by went in
that heathen hoard and took a cup
crusted with jewels. The dragon
soon found that in his sleep
he'd been tricked by the cunning thief.
Soon enough the neighbors knew
he was enraged.

The man who provoked him so sorely
didn't penetrate the dragon's hoard on purpose.
Somebody's servant, sin-busy, fleeing a flogging,
needed some shelter desperately. Stark terror
took hold of the intruder when he found
the horror within. Still, he made off with the cup.

Many such ancient treasures could be found
in that house of earth, where someone long ago
carefully hid the enormous legacy
of a noble race, their most precious belongings.
Death had carried them off long ago.

The song of the last survivor

The last surviving veteran of that troop,
mourning his lost friends, also knew
he had but little time
to enjoy that long-accumulated wealth.

On a meadow near the ocean's waves
there was a barrow, newly made and well protected,
standing on a cliff. The ring-guardian bore
the golden treasures worthy of keeping there
and said these words over the hoard:

"Earth, guard the wealth of princes,
now that men no longer can!
Indeed, men took it from you long ago.
Battle-death, deadly evil has taken
one and all: every man of my people
who once knew the joys of the hall
has let go of this life.

"No one to wield the sword
or offer the jeweled cup, the precious flagon.
The troop has departed. The hard helmet,
battle-grim, adorned with gold, has fallen—
the man who kept it bright
now sleeps. Likewise the coat of mail
that in battle over broken shields
endured the bite of steel
now molders like the man.

"No more will they follow their war chief,
standing staunch with heroes.
No more the joys of the harp,
the pleasure of its gleeful wood,
nor the good hawk swooping through the hall.
No more the swift horse
stamping in the courtyard.
Baleful slaughter has sent forth
so many living things!"

So mournfully he spoke his sorrow,
the one man left of them all,
joylessly passing his days
and nights until the tide
of death touched his heart.

The dragon inherits the hoard

An old raider of darkness,
smoldering, seeking out barrows,
found that wonderful hoard standing open—
a naked dragon, night flying,
furled in flames, filling the country folk
with fear. Old in winters, he sought out wealth
beneath the ground, guarding the heathen gold—
though he wasn't one whit better off
because of it.

That destroyer of men, huge and powerful,
held onto the hoard for three hundred years—
until someone enraged him, bearing a treasure cup
away to his lord to beg his pardon.
The hoard had been found out and plundered.
The lord forgave the wretched man
as soon as he laid eyes on that ancient work.

The worm's revenge

So the worm was awakened, and the trouble began.
Stalking among the rocks, he found
the bold-hearted criminal's tracks
where he cunningly crept past the dragon's head.
So may a man not doomed by fate
easily come through exile and woe
if God's grace protects him.

The hoard's guardian searched the ground eagerly.
He wanted to find the man
who brought him sorrow in his sleep.
Hot and furious, he circled the barrow
again and again, spoiling for a fight
but finding no one in that wasteland.
Time and again he turned back to the barrow
looking for his precious cup, but soon realized
someone had taken off with his golden treasure.

The hoard-guard bade his time bitterly
until evening came. The barrow's keeper was enraged.
He would reward the theft of his cup
with scorching fire.

The daylight failed, to the dragon's great delight.
He would not wait in the barrow any longer
but go forth in flames, urged onward by fire.
The onset of his attack
was as terrifying to the people
as its ending would be sorry
for their treasure-giver.

The demon began to spew forth flames
burning up the bright buildings
the light of fires rising
to the terror of men. The flying evil
would not leave anything alive.

Near and far, the war waged by the dragon
could be seen, his cruel assault,
how the destroyer hated and harried the Geats.
He returned to the hoard, his dark
and secret hall, before day's light.

Having engulfed the nation in fire and flames
he trusted the walls of his barrow
to protect him. That trust
would fail him.

Beowulf makes his plans

The news was quickly brought to Beowulf
that his own home, best of buildings,
gift-throne of the Geats,
had melted in the surging flames.

The good man's heart was filled with anguish,
the worst soul-sorrow. He imagined
he must have broken some ancient law,
bitterly angered God somehow.
His mind was filled with gloomy thoughts,
which was not his habit.

The fire-dragon had razed the people's fortress,
consuming the seacoast in flames.
The Weather-Geats' lord and war-king
carefully planned his revenge.
The people's protector
ordered a splendid shield made
all of steel—he knew well that linden wood
was no help against this fire.

The king, having ruled long and well,
awaited the end of the passing days
of this world's life. And the dragon,
however long it had held its hoarded wealth,
was going with him.

The ring-lord had too much pride
to seek out the wide-flying dragon
with a great troop of men.
He had no fear of the fight,
nor did he care one whit
for the worm's fighting force,
its strength and valor.

After all, he had survived
some tight spots before, braving
the clash of battle, blessed with victory
ever since he cleansed Hrothgar's hall
grappling with Grendel's hateful kin.

Recalling Hygelac's fall

Nor was that a small affair
where Hygelac was slain. The king of Geats,
friend of his people, Hrethel's son
died in a battle rush in Friesland—
sword blades drank his blood.

Then Beowulf by strength and skill
crossed over the ocean waves.
With thirty enemy mail shirts in his arms
he set back out to sea.

The Hetware had no call to boast
about that battle.
They attacked Beowulf, bearing shields,
but few of them went back home
after facing that fighter.

Beowulf helps Hygelac's son, Heardred

Swimming over the seal's wide realm
Ecgtheow's son returned to his people
alone and filled with grief.
There, Queen Hygd offered him the kingdom
and the treasure hoard, the rings and throne.
She did not trust that her own young child
could defend the country from foreign enemies
now that Hygelac lay dead.

But still the unfortunate nation
could not by any means convince
this noble hero to be Heardred's lord
or choose to take the throne.
Instead he supported Heardred loyally
with friendly counsel, kindness, help
until the child was old enough
to rule the Weather-Geats.

Onela kills Heardred. Beowulf's revenge

Some wretched outcasts, sons of Ohthere
sought out Heardred over the seas.
They had rebelled against Onela,
famed lord of the Scylfings, best of the sea-kings
who gave out rings in Sweden.

That spelled the end for Heardred.
The reward he got for his hospitality
was a mortal wound—
a sword-stroke for the son of Hygelac.

Once Heardred lay dead, Onela
son of Ongentheow went home,
leaving Beowulf to take the throne
and rule the Geats. He made a good king.

For a long time Beowulf kept in mind
vengeance for the killing of his king.
He befriended Eadgils in his exile,
supplying the son of Ohthere
with warriors and weapons.
After a cold, hard conflict
he got revenge, took king Onela's life.

And so he survived every struggle,
each vicious attack and deed of valor,
until the day arrived to fight the dragon.

They set out to find the dragon

Twelve of them went, including
the king of the Geats, enraged by grief,
to look for the dragon. He had found out
how the feud arose, this baleful affliction
of his people. The notorious jeweled cup
had been laid in his lap by an informer.

The thirteenth member of the troop
was the unhappy slave who had started the feud.
The wretch had to point out the place.
Against his will he was going back
to that hall of earth he alone knew of,
the underground barrow
close by the ocean's crashing waves.

Inside, it was filled with ornaments and filigree.
A terrible guardian, ready for battle
protected those golden treasures,
old under the earth. It was no easy business
for any man to get it.

The battle-hard king sat down on the cliff.
The gold-friend of the Geats
wished his companions health and prosperity.
He was sad at heart, restless
and ready for death. His fated doom
was drawing near. Soon it would seek him out,
sacking his soul's treasure hoard,

splitting life from limb. Not much longer now
would that prince's soul be wrapped in flesh.

Beowulf reviews his life

Beowulf, son of Ecgtheow, spoke:
"In my youth I came through many battle charges,
times of war—I remember it all.
I was seven winters old when my treasure lord,
friend of the people, took me from my father.
King Hrethel raised and fostered me
offering feasts and treasure, keeping our kinship in mind.
Grown to manhood in his house,
I was no less dear to him than his own sons,
Herebeald, Haethcyn, or my lord Hygelac.

Herebeald's tragic death and Hrethel's grief

"An untimely deathbed was laid out for the eldest
through his own kinsman's deed
when Haethcyn, with his horn bow
struck down his friend with an arrow,
missed his mark and shot his closest kin,
one brother's blood upon the other's shaft.

"It was a crime blood money could not cleanse,
a sin to baffle the weary mind.
But there it was—a prince had lost his life
and could never be avenged.

"It was sad as an old man seeing
his young son swinging from the gallows.
He utters a song of sorrow
as his son hangs there, food for the ravens
and he, so old and wise, cannot help him at all.

"Each and every morning he remembers
his son's distant journey. He has no wish to wait
for another heir in his house, when the first
has been forced to taste death.
He gazes in sorrow at his son's old home,
the wine-hall deserted, a wind-swept resting place

bereft of joy. The rider sleeps,
the hero hidden in his grave.

"No more the sound of the harp
in the hall, of games in the yard
as there used to be. The one takes to his bed
singing a sorrow-song for the other.
The fields and the house feel too big for him.

"So the Weder king's heart overflowed
with sorrow for Herebeald
but there was no way to settle the feud
with his killer. He could not hate
his son for this terrible deed
but neither could he love him any longer.

"The sorrow was too bitter to endure—
he gave up the joys of men and chose God's light.
He gave his heirs, like any prosperous man
his lands and towns when he left this life.

Hygelac becomes king

"There was strife between Swedes and Geats—
bitter quarrels broke out, hard war-hate
over the wide waters, after Hrethel's death.
The sons of Ongentheow were bold and warlike;
they would not keep the peace across the sea.
Time and again they carried out terrible slaughters
around Hreosnabeorh.

"My kinsmen avenged those quarrels and crimes,
as everyone knows. But one of them paid for it
with his life, a hard bargain:
Haethcyn, lord of the Geats, fell in battle.

"The next morning, as I've heard, the other brother
saw a sword's edge settle the account
when Ongentheow sought out Eofor in battle.
His helmet split wide, the old Scylfing king
fell, pale from the sword. Eofor's hand
remembered their quarrel well enough—
he didn't hold back on that deadly swing.

Beowulf becomes his champion

"Hygelac gave me land, the pleasures
of a great estate. I repaid the treasures he gave me
as best I could with a bright sword in battle.
He had no need to look to the Gifthas,
the Spear-Danes or to Sweden,
offer treasure for a lesser warrior.

"I would always go before him,
alone at the point, in the forefront of his troops.
And I will go on fighting as long as my life
and my good sword lasts. It has always
stood by me since that time,
in front of the whole host, I slew Daeghrefne,
the Huga champion, in hand-to-hand combat.

"He would bring back no treasure and armor
to his Frisian king. Their standard-bearer,
brave and noble, crumpled in the field.
It was no blade's edge that killed him—
my war-grip stopped the surging of his heart
and broke his house of bone.

"Now the sword's edge,
hand and hard blade
must do battle for the hoard."

Last vows

For the last time
Beowulf spoke his battle vows:
"I did a lot of fighting in my youth.
Now, an aged guardian of my people,
I'm still willing to seek out combat,
to do a great deed, if the mankiller
in that cave comes out to find me."

He addressed to his beloved comrades,
each brave man who bore a helmet,
these final words:

"I would not wear a sword,
nor take a weapon to that worm,
if there were any way to come to grips
with the monster, as I did with Grendel.
But I expect a blast of fire,
boiling, poisonous breath, and so
I must bear a shield and armor.

"I will not flee so much as a foot
from the guardian of this barrow.
By this wall we will find out
what fate has been assigned us
by the Creator of every man.

"My mind is firm.
I will speak no more vows
about that war-flyer. Wait here
behind the barrow, protected by your armor
to see which of the two of us
better survives his wounds from the battle rush.

"This is not your adventure,
nor fitting for any man but me
to try his strength against the monster,
do this noble deed. By my own valor
I will either win gold
or else war, brave death in battle
will take your king!"

The fight with the dragon

The famed warrior arose with his shield.
Hard under helmet, he bore his chain mail
beneath the stone cliff, trusting to his strength alone.
This was no job for a coward. The best of men,
who had endured so many hardships
in war, so many clashes of soldiers,
could see a stone arch in the barrow's wall.

A stream of fire
burst forth from the barrow—
surging and rushing waves of flame.

No man could approach the hoard unburned,
endure for a moment the barrow's depths
because of the dragon's flaming breath.

The lord of the Weather-Geats, enraged
let words fly forth from his breast.
The staunch heart gave a battle shout—
ringing and clear, his voice carried far
beneath the hoary stone.

The dragon's hatred was aroused:
the hoard-guard knew that voice to be a man.
The time for seeking peace was past.
Immediately, the monster's breath
flared forth from the stone, hot battle roar,
and the ground resounded.

Close by the barrow
the Geat lord raised his shield
against his terrifying guest.
The coiled creature's heart
was on fire for battle.
The great war-king had already drawn his sword,
an ancient heirloom whose edge was not dull.
Both intent on destruction, each one
was in horror of the other.

The lord of warriors stood staunchly
with his shield, waiting in his armor
as the worm quickly coiled itself together.
Once fully wound, the scalding creature
slithered and struck out, rushing to its fate.

His shield would not protect
the life and limbs of that famous lord
as long as his heart had wished.
This was the first time he had to face
that fate would not grant him victory in battle.

The Geat lord's hand swung upward
and struck at the glittering terror
but the bright edge bit the bone

more weakly than its lord had need of now,
hard-pressed and in trouble.

After that battle-stroke, the barrow's guardian
was furious, spewing war-flames,
murderous fire everywhere.
The gold-friend of the Geats
was not boasting of victory now—
his naked war-blade failed him in his need
as it never should have, the steel
that had always been tried and true.

Nor was that an easy journey
the great son of Ecgtheow
now had to make—giving up this ground
and going to dwell in a different place,
returning, as every man must, these borrowed days.

It wasn't long
before he clashed with the dragon again.
The hoard's guardian took new heart,
his chest swelled with breath again.
The man who had once ruled a nation
now suffered in agony, wrapped in flames.

His companions abandon him—all but one

None of his hand-picked companions,
sons of nobles, stood by him now.
They had run away to the woods
to save their lives. But one among them
now felt sorrow welling in his chest.
Nothing can change the bonds of kinship
for a right-thinking man.

This man's name was Wiglaf
Weohstan's son, a worthy shield-bearer
and Scylfing prince, Aelfhere's kinsman.
When he saw his lord suffering
such heat beneath his helmet, he remembered
the honors that his king had given him,
the rich estate of the Waegmundings

and other rights and holdings he enjoyed
like his father before him.

Then he could not hold back—
he grabbed his shield of yellow linden wood
and grasped his ancient sword.

It was the heirloom of Eanmund, Ohtere's son.
Weohstan had killed this friendless outlaw
in battle, brought his war gear
to his kinsman: bright helmet, shirt of ring mail
and the sword, an ancient work of giants.

King Onela gave him back the gear,
the battle-ready armor, saying not a word
about a feud, although the man slain
was the son of his brother.

He held onto that sword and armor many years
until his son was ready for heroic deeds
like his father before him. Then, among the Geats,
he gave him all that war gear
before the old man left his life, went on his way.

This was the first time the young champion
would charge into battle beside his lord.
When they met, the worm would find out
that Wiglaf's courage would not melt,
nor his father's gift prove weak in battle.

Wiglaf encourages the others

Wiglaf, grieved at heart,
spoke fitting words to his companions:
"I remember a time we were drinking mead
in his hall. We promised our lord,
the giver of these rings, we would repay him
for this war equipment, helmets and hard swords
if he ever had a time of need like this.

"He chose us freely for this mission
from among the troops, considered us
worthy of glory and gave us treasure

because he accounted us good spearmen,
brave helmet-bearers—although our lord
planned to accomplish this heroic work alone,
since he had more fame for wildly daring deeds
than any other man.

"Now the day has come
when our lord needs the strength of good soldiers.
Let us go to him, help our commander
as long as this fire-terror lasts!
As for me, God knows I had rather
let my body be embraced by flame
beside my gold-giver.

"It doesn't seem right to me
that we should bear our shields back home
before we stop the enemy and save
the life of the lord of the Weather-Geats.
I know for a fact that, after all he's done,
he does not deserve to be the only one
of all the Geats to suffer agony
and fall in battle. Let's share our swords and helmets,
chain mail and armor with him!"

Wiglaf joins Beowulf

He waded into the deadly, reeking smoke
bearing his helmet to his master's aid,
saying only this: "Beloved Beowulf,
make good on those words
you spoke so eagerly in your youth—
that as long as you lived
you would never let your glory fail.
So now my lord, be brave and resolute,
use every ounce of strength to save your life.
I will be right beside you!"

After these words the dragon—furious,
terrible foe wreathed in surging flame—
attacked its enemies again, the men it hated.
A wave of fire burned Wiglaf's shield
right down to the boss. His chain mail was no help either.

The young man took cover under his kinsman's shield
after his own was burned to ashes.

The final struggle

Once more the war-king, his mind set on glory,
struck out with his sword, putting all his strength behind it.
It stuck in the dragon's head, driven in by sheer force—
but then the great sword Naegling burst.
Beowulf's gray and ancient weapon
failed him in battle.

It was not his fate that any iron weapon
would help at war—his hand was too strong,
his swing asked too much of any blade
he bore into battle. According to what I hear,
no matter how wondrously hard the weapon,
it did him not one whit of good.

Now for a third time the mankiller,
the terrible fire dragon, intended to attack.
Seeing his chance, he rushed in
hot and battle-grim, grabbing Beowulf's neck
in his bitter fangs. The man was drenched
in his life-blood, surging out.

Then, as I have heard, in his king's great need
the man beside him made his courage known,
the strength and boldness he was born with.
Paying no heed to the dragon's head,
burning his hand to help his kinsman,
he struck the strange creature a little farther down—
the fierce and finely-crafted sword sank in
and the fire began to grow dim.

Now the king came back to his senses.
He drew a long dagger, bitter, battle-sharp
from his chain mail, and cut the worm
clean through the belly.

They had killed the enemy.
Their courage had sent its soul
into exile. And they had done it together,
the two noble kinsmen. That's how a man
should act, a thane in time of need!
For the lord, it was the last time
he would win victory by his deeds,
the last of his works in this world.

The dragon wound

The wound the earth-dragon had given him
began to burn and swell. Soon he could feel
the deadly poison welling in his breast.

The wise prince went to sit by the wall.
He could see the stone arches, the work of giants,
supported by pillars inside that eternal stone hall.

Then the good thane, with his own hands
washed his blood-stained lord with water,
unclasped the helmet of his friend and master,
weary and sick of battle.

Beowulf looks back on his time as king

Beowulf spoke, despite his mortal wound.
He knew well he had lived out his daytime,
his joys on this earth. The count of his days
was completed, his death immeasurably near.

"I would have wished to leave my war gear
to a son of mine, an heir of my body
to succeed me, if I had been granted one.
I ruled my people fifty winters
and no neighboring king ever dared
to threaten terror, or attack me
with warriors. I lived my allotted time
on earth, protected well what was mine,
never engaging in treacherous quarrels
nor swearing a lot of false oaths.

"Now, sick with my mortal wound,
I can take comfort in all of that.
I know the Ruler of men will have no need
to accuse me of murdering kinsmen
when my life leaves my body.

"Beloved Wiglaf, please hurry
and show me the hoard underneath the gray stone,
now that the dragon sleeps, sorely wounded
and bereft of treasure. Be quick now
so that I can see that ancient wealth,
gaze on that gold, those glittering jewels.
So that after seeing that treasure trove
I can let go more easily
the life and lordship that I held so long."

Wiglaf shows him the treasure

Then, I have heard, the son of Weohstan
quickly obeyed the words of his wounded lord,
went in his ring mail, his woven battle shirt
beneath the barrow's roof. Going past the seat
the brave thane saw gleams of yellow,
gold glittering on the ground,
wonders hung on the wall.

In the den of the dragon, the old night-flyer
he saw cups and pitchers, the flagons of men of old
with none to polish them, their jewels all fallen.
There was many a helmet, old and rusty,
armbands in abundance, skillfully twisted.
Gold in the ground, buried treasure
can easily overpower any man,
let him hide it who will.

Likewise he saw a standard all of gold
hanging high above the hoard.
A hand-woven wonder, it cast a light
by which he could see the treasure on the floor.
No sign of the worm—the sword's edge
had carried him away.

Then I heard the man began to plunder
the barrow, that ancient work of giants,
loading his bosom with drinking cups and plates
of his own choosing, taking the standard too,
the brightest of banners.

For the iron edge of his old lord's knife
had killed the one who guarded the hoard
so long, waging a war of fire-terror
at midnight, blasting hot and fierce
for the sake of the hoard
until he was slaughtered himself.

Urged on by the treasure he carried
the messenger hurried, eager to get back.
He was bursting with anxiety to know
whether the Geat lord, sick and sapped of strength
was still alive where he had left him.

Treasures in hand, he found his famous king
blood-soaked, coming to his end.
Once more, he splashed him with water
until the sharp point of a word
broke out of the hoard in his breast.
Seeing the gold, the king spoke through his pain:

Last words and wishes. Death of Beowulf.

"For all this treasure, I thank the Lord
the King of Glory, the Eternal Ruler
that I can gaze upon it now—that I was able,
before I died, to win such riches for my people.
I bought this treasure with my old life.
Take care of my people now—
I cannot last much longer.

"After the funeral pyre
have my brave soldiers build a shining barrow
on a point above the sea
towering high over Hronesnesse.
It will serve as a reminder for my people
so that sailors ever after, driving their ships

far across the dark ocean
will call it Beowulf's barrow."

The brave lord took the golden collar
from his neck and gave his thane,
the young spearman, his golden helmet,
rings and mail shirt, told him to use them well.
"You are the last of our kin, the Waegmundings.
Fate has swept away my family. Brave and noble,
all have gone to meet their destiny
and I must follow them."

Those were the old man's very last words,
the thoughts of his heart, before he would embrace
the hot, fierce flames of his funeral pyre.
His soul departed from his breast
to seek the judgment of the true and just.

Wiglaf is left alone

It was hard for the young man
seeing that most beloved life
end there on the ground,
after suffering so much.

The killer also lay there:
the terrible earth-dragon
was destroyed, bereft of life.
The worm's wicked coils
would guard the hoard no longer.

An iron edge carried him off,
hard and battle-sharp, the hammer's heirloom.
So the wide-flyer, stilled by his wounds,
fell to earth near his treasure house. Never again
would he whirl through the midnight air,
making a show of himself,
proud in possession of his riches.
He was brought down to earth
by that warrior's handwork.

Indeed, there are few mighty men on this earth
that I have heard of, no matter how daring,
who could brave the breath of a poison foe,
run his hands through its treasure,
if he found the guardian awake inside its barrow.
Beowulf paid for that princely treasure
with his death—both of them brought to the end
of this passing life.

Those who fled now return

It wasn't long
before those who had fled the battle
came out of the woods—
spineless oath-breakers, ten of them altogether,
who had not dared to let their spears fly
in their lord's great need. Shamefully
they bore their shields and battle gear
back to where the old man lay,
and gazed at Wiglaf.

The brave champion sat, exhausted,
by the shoulder of his lord
trying to waken him with water.
He had no success at all:
no matter how much he wished it,
he could not keep his battle-lord's life
on this earth, nor overrule the Ruler in the least.
God's judgment determined the deeds
of every man, as He still does.

Those who had lost their courage
found it easy to get a grim reply
from that young man. Wiglaf son of Weohstan,
wounded at heart, looked upon them with loathing:

"Well, a man who wants to tell the truth can surely say
that the lord who gave you treasure
and the fighting gear you stand there in,
when on the ale-benches he gave his hall-troops
helmets and mail shirts, the best he could find
from far and near for his thanes—one can say

he completely and utterly threw all that war gear away
when the actual war came upon him.

"No, our king cannot boast
of those who stood by him in battle.
But God, the King of victory
granted that he could avenge himself
alone with the edge of his blade,
when he had need of courage.

"I could do little to shield his life
in battle. Still, although it was beyond my measure,
I did what little I could to help my kinsman.
After I struck the dragon with my sword
the fire surged weaker and weaker
from the head of our deadly foe.
Too few defenders thronged about our lord
when his time of hardship came.

"But now gifts of treasure and swords,
the joys and comforts of home
will end for your families
and all your kin—every man of them
must give up his land rights, abandon his estates
and leave them empty when noblemen everywhere
find out about your flight, your shameful deed.
To any noble warrior, death is better
than a life of disgrace!"

Announcing the terrible news

He ordered the battle-work to be announced
at the stronghold on the cliff's edge,
where the band of warriors had sat, dejected,
all morning by their shields, expecting
either the beloved man's return
or the end of his days.
The one who rode across the headland
was not silent about the news
but spoke out truthfully to all:

"Now is the joy-giver of the Weder people,
the lord of the Geats, laid fast on his deathbed,
lying slaughtered by the dragon's deed.
His life's enemy lies beside him, sick with knife stabs—
his sword could not wound that monster in any way.
Wiglaf son of Weohstan sits beside him, grieving,
keeping death watch over friend and foe.

Feuds and forebodings

"Now our nation can expect a time of war
once our king's fall is widely known
to the Franks and the Frisians. The hard feud
against the Hugas began when Hygelac
sailed with his war fleet to Frisia.
There the Hetware fell upon him
and with courage and greater strength
made that mailed warrior bow to earth,
fall amidst his foot soldiers. That lord
would give no treasure to his troops.
Ever since, the Merovingian kings
have shown us no mercy.

The Battle of Ravenwood: Hygelac avenges the death of Haethcyn

"Nor do I expect any peace
or pledge of friendship from the Swedes.
It's well known that Ongentheow took the life
of Haethcyn, Hrethel's son, at Ravenwood
where the Geats, out of arrogant pride
first attacked the War-Scylfings.

"The wise father of Ohthere,
old and terrible, soon paid them back—
he slew the leader of the seamen
and rescued his old wife, the mother
of Onela and Ohthere, bereft of her jewels.
He pursued his deadly foe until they escaped,
with difficulty and without their lord,
into Ravenwood.

"With a huge army, he laid siege
to the sword's survivors, weary of their wounds.
He threatened the miserable band all night
saying when the morning came
the sword's edge would destroy them
and he would hang some on the gallows tree
for the ravens to play with.

"But help came before daylight
for the heartsick men. They heard the sound
of Hygelac's horns and trumpets—
the good man was coming down the trail
with his veteran troops.

"Such was the bloody swath cut out
by the Swedes and Geats, the well-known slaughter,
the way the nations stirred up a feud between them.

The Swedes retreat

"The wise old king and his companions,
filled with regret, sought out his fortress.
The noble Ongentheow withdrew. He had heard
of Hygelac's bold warcraft, and did not believe
that he could resist the seamen, protect
his hoard, his women and children
against the raiders. So he retreated,
old behind his wall of earth.

"Pursuit of the Swedish host was called for.
The banners of Hygelac overran their ranks,
the men of Hrethel thronging around their walls.
There the gray-haired Ongentheow was brought to bay
by sharp blades; the king was at Eofor's mercy.

"Wulf son of Wonred angrily struck him with his weapon,
a stroke that made the blood spring from the veins
beneath his hair. But the old Scylfing felt no fear
because of that—he quickly spun round
and paid back that murderous blow
with a worse one.

"The bold son of Wonred could not strike back
at the old man now—Ongentheow
had sheared through the helmet on his head
so he had to bow down, drenched in blood,
and fell to earth. But he was not doomed yet:
he would recover, though sorely hurt.

Eofor avenges his brother

"With his brother lying on the ground, Eofor,
stout thane of Hygelac, lifted his broad sword,
old blade made by giants, broke through the shield wall
and brought it down on Ongentheow's giant helm.
The king crumpled over, cut to the quick.

"Once they had won that field of slaughter
many rushed to bind his brother's wounds
and lift him up. As one warrior to another
Eofor plundered Ongentheow's body
taking his iron mail, his hard, hilted sword
and his helmet too.

"He carried the graybeard's gear to Hygelac.
Taking those treasures, the Geat lord graciously promised
to reward him. When he got home, Hrethel's son
fulfilled his promise. In return for their battle charge,
he gave Wulf and Eofor enormous treasure:
a hundred thousand worth in land and rings. No man
on this middle earth needs to blame him for that—
they had won glory in battle. And to Eofor,
as a pledge of friendship, he gave his only daughter
to grace his home.

"So deep is that feud and enmity,
murderous hatred among men,
that I expect the Swedes will seek us out
when they find our lord lifeless,
the one who guarded our hoard and home
against all enemies. After our other heroes,
brave shield-bearers, had fallen
he did what was best for our people
performing a hero's deeds.

The fate of the hoard and the Geats

"Now haste is best—
let us look upon our king
and take him who once gave us rings
on the path to his funeral pyre.
Nor shall just a token of that treasure
melt with that brave-hearted man,
but the whole hoard, gold uncounted
grimly purchased—in the end
he bought those rings with his life.

"Burning brands shall devour them
under a roof thatched with fire.
No man shall wear these treasures
in his memory, no lovely maid
adorn her neck with rings.
But grieving and bereft of gold
they will be treading strange lands
not once, but often, now that our war-chief
has laid aside laughter, joy and mirth.

"Many a morning-cold spear
shall be grasped in our fists,
raised high in our hands.
It will not be the sound of the harp
that wakes the warriors, but the dark raven,
ready and waiting above the doomed.
He will have much to say to the eagle
about how he fared at the feast
when he plundered the dead with the wolf."

They go to see their king

So the brave man told them the terrible news,
not lying as to words or deeds. The troop
stood up and made their way, weary of soul
under the Eagle's Cliff, tears welling up
at the awful sight. They found there,
resting upon the sand, bereft of soul
the one who had given them rings in days gone by.
The end of the good man's days had come.

The war-king of the Weather-Geats
had died a strange and wondrous death.

But first they saw a stranger being—
the worm that lay there on the ground
in front of its enemy. The flaming dragon,
fifty feet in length, was grimly stained
and scorched with fire.
It once had the joy of the sky all night
before it descended to seek its den.
Now death held it fast.
It needed its cave no more.

Beside the dragon were drinking cups and flagons,
dishes, plates and precious swords
eaten up with rust, just as they had lain
for a thousand winters in the earth's embrace.
That heirloom gold of men long gone
was wound about with a mighty spell
so that no man could touch that hall of rings
unless God himself, Protector of men, true King of victory
granted someone he saw fit
to open that hoard.

Clearly, things had not gone well
for the one who had wrongfully, secretly kept
the treasure within these walls. Its guardian
had killed quite a few, but that feud
had been fiercely avenged.

It is a mystery
where a brave and noble man
may meet his fated end,
when he may no longer dwell
with his men in the mead hall.
So it was with Beowulf
when he took up his dangerous quarrel
against the guardian of the barrow—
he knew not what
would bring about his parting from this world.

The treasure was deeply cursed until Doomsday came
by the illustrious lords who placed it there
so that the man who set foot within
would be guilty of sin, confined to demon haunts,
tormented, held fast in the shackles of Hell,
unless the gold-seeker had indeed
found favor with God beforehand.

Wiglaf shows them the hoard

Wiglaf, son of Weohstan, spoke:
"Often many will suffer misfortune
through the will of one, as has happened to us.
We could not convince our beloved lord,
our nation's protector, by any kind of counsel
not to attack the guardian of the gold,
to let him lie there, as he had so long
until the end of the world.
But he held to his high destiny—
the hoard is discovered
and grimly won. The fate was too strong
that drove him there.

"I went inside and saw it all,
that hall's precious goods—no easy entrance
was granted me under that earthen wall.
I quickly grabbed a heavy load
of hoarded treasure, and took it to my king.

"He was still alive, and sound
of mind and sense. The old man
spoke much in his pain.
He bade me greet you,
asking that you build
on the place of his funeral pyre
a high barrow, glorious and grand,
befitting the deeds of your friend.
For he was the worthiest warrior
upon this wide earth, for as long
as he enjoyed his stronghold's wealth.

"Now let us hurry once again
to seek out that pile of rarest gems,
that wonder under the walls. I'll show the way
so you can see for yourself, up close
the broad gold and the rings.

"Let the bier be made ready,
the pyre prepared when we come out
bearing the body of our lord, that beloved man
to the place where he shall long abide
in the Master's keeping."

Then the son of Weohstan, hale warrior
bade it be announced that every man
who owned a house should bring in wood
from far and near for the funeral pyre.

"Now shall fire and smoke rise up
and flames devour the prince of warriors,
he who so often endured the showers of iron,
storms of arrows sped from bowstrings
flying over the shield wall—
eager shafts, clad in their feathered gear
speeding the arrowheads onward."

Quickly the wise son of Weohstan
chose the seven best thanes from the troop
and the eight of them entered
beneath that evil roof. The first in line
carried a torch in his hand. There was no need
to draw lots to plunder that hoard. The men
saw everything lying loose, unguarded
and neglected. No one was sorry
to quickly carry out those precious treasures.

The dragon's body they shoved
over the sea cliff, let the waves
have the worm, the flood's embrace
take the treasure-keeper.

Beowulf's funeral pyre

A countless quantity of twisted gold
was laden in the wagon.
Then the noble prince
the gray warrior
was borne to Hronesnesse.

The Geats prepared for him a mighty pyre
hung with shields and helmets and bright armor
as he had asked. In its midst, the grieving heroes
laid their beloved lord.

Up on the cliff, the men awakened
the greatest of bael-fires.
Wood smoke rose black
above the blaze, the roaring flames
surrounded by weeping, whipped
by wind, until the fire
broke into his house of bones,
burning hot around his heart.

With heavy hearts the Geats
gave voice to their sorrow
over the killing of their king.
So sadly an old woman sang,
her hair bound up, a song of mourning,
in her grief cried again and again
she feared hard days ahead
slaughter and the terror of war
shame and slavery.

Heaven swallowed the smoke.

Beowulf's barrow

Then the Weather-Geats built a great barrow
upon the headland, made it high and broad,
a sight for seafarers far away.

In ten days' time
they raised the brave man's monument
upon the ashes of his pyre,

working those walls as splendidly
as the wisest craftsmen could devise.

Inside the barrow they placed the rings and jewels
and all such ornaments as warlike men
had taken from the hoard.
Into the keeping of the earth
they gave the noble treasure,
gold in the ground, where it lies
to this day, as useless to men
as it had been before.

Around his barrow
rode brave and noble princes,
twelve in all, to speak their sorrow
mourn the king and sing a dirge
about the man, praising his heroic deeds
his power and his works of courage.
For it is fitting that a man
should praise his lord with heartfelt love
when he has to take leave of his body.

And so the Geat people grieved their lord's fall
along with his hearth companions
saying that he, of all the world's kings
was the most kind and gentle
the most gracious to his people
the most eager for everlasting fame.

The Finnsburg Fragment

The "Fight at Finnsburg," part of which is sung at a feast in *Beowulf*, existed as an independent poem. We still have this fragment of the original, which takes place before the part in *Beowulf* begins. From what we can reconstruct of the situation, the Danish princess Hildeburg has been given to the Frisian king Finn in marriage, evidently as a "peace-weaver" to help mend a feud. Her brother Hnaef, now the Danish king, comes to visit her at Finn's fortress. The feud flares up again; Hnaef and his men are treacherously attacked at night.

In the *Beowulf* version, Hengest becomes the leader of the Danes after Hnaef is killed. Intriguingly, tradition says that the first Anglo-Saxon chieftains to come to England were Hengist and Horsa. Given the fluidity of tribal alliances (and spelling) in those days, it's possible that this Hengest is the very same man. The "people's leader" at the end of this fragment is probably Finn himself, asking a wounded warrior how the Danes inside the hall were doing. As we learn in *Beowulf*, they were holding up better than Finn had hoped.

The Danes see a strange light

Hnaef, a king young in battle, cried out:
"That is not day dawning in the east,
nor a dragon flying,
nor the [horns of this hall] burning.
But the birds are screaming
and the gray-coated creature howls.
War-wood rings out:
shield answering shaft of spear.

"Now the moon shines,
wandering behind the clouds.
Now will dreadful deeds be done
to carry out the hatred of this people.

"Awake now, my warriors!
Grab hold of your linden shields.
Set your mind on deeds of valor.
Fight in the front rank, be brave!"

Many a thane in trappings of gold
arose now and strapped on his sword.
Sigeferth and Eaha, noble champions,
went to the door with drawn blades.
At the other door, Ordlaf and Guthlaf
with Hengest himself in their tracks.

Outside the door, the attackers confer

Garulf urged Guthere not to risk
his noble life, nor bear
his beautiful armor to that hall door
where someone determined to do him harm
would take it. But the brave-hearted hero
shouted out clearly above them all
asking who held the door to the hall.

"Sigeferth is my name," the warrior said.
"I am one of the Secgan people,
a well-known wanderer. I have come
through many hardships, bitter battles.
You'll soon find out what happens
when you come looking for me!"

Then the hall was roaring with shouts and slaughter.
Curved shields, bone-helmets
burst in the hands of keen warriors.
The fortress floor resounded
until Garulf son of Guthlaf,
first among the native troops,
crumpled in the fight. Around him
many good men fell,
turned into twisted corpses.

The raven circled, dark and dusky.
Sword-light flashed
as if all Finnsburg were on fire.

Never have I heard of sixty men
who bore themselves better in battle,
or with greater honor. Never have young men
paid better for their shining mead
than Hnaef's men repaid him for theirs.

They fought for five days.
Not one of the retainers fell
and still they held the door.

Then a wounded warrior turned to go
saying his armor was broken
his war gear useless and his helmet pierced.

The people's leader quickly questioned him
about how those warriors bore their wounds

and whether the young men....
(the fragment ends here)

Selected Readings & Media

Beowulf : manuscript and electronic resources

British Museum *Beowulf* Manuscript http://www.bl.uk/manuscripts/FullDisplay.aspx?ref=Cotton_MS_vitellius_a_xv
Complete Beowulf manuscript viewable online in high-resolution photography.
Click the bottom folio (Cotton MS Vitellius A XV, ff 94r–209v) and go to page 132r.

Beowulf Resources Online http://beowulfresources.com
An impressive collection of links to Beowulf manuscripts, translations, criticism and history.

Electronic Beowulf: Third Edition (Multimedia CD-ROM) Kevin Kiernan (British Library, 2011)
Includes all transcripts and emendations, ultraviolet photos of the manuscript, glossary and grammar. Overview and guide online at *Electronic Beowulf* http://ebeowulf.uky.edu

Beowulf: Reproduced in Facsimile from the Unique Manuscript, British Museum Ms. Cotton Vitellius A. Xv Second edition, Julius Zupitza, editor (Early English Text Society, Oxford U. Press, 1959). Print.
Photographs of the complete manuscript with facing transliteration.

Beowulf : text

Beowulf Klaeber, Third edition with first and second supplements (D.C. Heath, 1950)
Long the standard scholarly edition, with extensive notes and glossary.

Klaeber's Beowulf Fourth edition, edited by R. D. Fulk, Robert E. Bjork, and John D. Niles
(Toronto Old English Series, U. of Toronto Press, 2008)
An update of Klaeber's classic text, incorporating current scholarship and textual studies.

Beowulf : translations

Beowulf Howell D. Chickering, Jr. (Anchor Books, 2006)
Excellent verse translation with facing Anglo-Saxon text and extensive notes.

Beowulf and Other Old English Poems Constance B. Hieatt (Bantam, 2008)
Faithful prose translations of the best-known Anglo-Saxon poems.

Beowulf: An Illustrated Edition Seamus Heaney (W.W. Norton, 2008)
This popular verse translation is brilliantly poetic at times. But it misses some of the inherent poetry of the original, and, as a personal touch, uses many obscure expressions from the poet's rural Ulster childhood.

Beowulf : background and criticism

A Beowulf Handbook Robert E. Bjork and John D. Niles, editors (U. of Nebraska Press, 1998)
A substantial compendium of Beowulf scholarship over the years, addressing all the major issues.

Beowulf R.W. Chambers (Cambridge U. Press, 1963)
Excellent source for background material on the poem's sources and origins.

The Monsters and the Critics J.R.R. Tolkien (HarperCollins, 2007)
Tolkien's seminal and often-reprinted essay on *Beowulf* stresses its artistic integrity and literary value.

The Beowulf Poet Donald K. Fry, ed. (Prentice-Hall, 1968)
Presents the debate over the poet and the poem's composition.

The Audience of Beowulf Dorothy Whitelock (Oxford U. Press, 1964)
The social conditions of the poem's composition and performance.

A Companion to Beowulf Ruth Johnston Staver (Greenwood Press, 2005)
One of many "companions" to the poem, readable and inviting.

Finn and Hengist J.R.R. Tolkien, edited by Alan Bliss (Firebird Distributing, 1998)
Background to the Finnsburg episode in *Beowulf* and the Germanic world at the time of the Anglo-Saxon invasion of England.

Anglo-Saxon Language and Poetry

The Anglo-Saxon Poetic Records Krapp and Dobbie, editors (Columbia U. Press, 1961)
The standard edition of the complete body of Anglo-Saxon poetry.

Bright's Old English Grammar & Reader Cassidy and Ringler, editors (Holt, Rinehart, 1971)
An update of Bright's *Anglo-Saxon Reader* including prose excerpts and many of the minor poems.

Old English Reader Murray McGillivray (Broadview Press, 2011)
Includes poetry and prose. The companion online site has a very useful clickable glossary: http://people.ucalgary.ca/~mmcgilli/OEReader/

Riddles

The Exeter Book Riddles Kevin Crossley-Holland (Enitharmon Press, 2009)
Translations of most of the Exeter Book riddles, in poetic and good-humored verse.

Storm, and Other Old English Riddles Kevin Crossley-Holland (Farrar, Strauss, 1970)
A briefer selection of his excellent translations.

Anglo-Saxon Riddles of the Exeter Book Paul F. Baum (Duke U. Press, 1963)

A Feast of Creatures Craig Williamson (U. of Pennsylvania Press, 1982)

The Anglo-Saxon Genesis

The Junius Manuscript George Philip Krapp, editor (Columbia U. Press, 1969)
Anglo-Saxon texts of Genesis A, Genesis B, Exodus, Daniel, and *Christ and Satan.*

The Caedmon Poems Charles W. Kennedy, translator (Peter Smith, 1965)
The Junius Manuscript translated into English prose.

The Venerable Bede

Bede's Ecclesiastical History of the English Nation David Knowles, translator (E.P. Dutton, 1965)
Fascinating account of early English history from the viewpoint of AD 700.

Baedae Opera Historica J.E. King, translator (Loeb Classical Library, W. Heine-
mann, Ltd., 1962)
Bede's original Latin with facing English translation.

Anglo-Saxon England

The Anglo-Saxon World: An Anthology Kevin Crossley-Holland (Oxford World's
Classics, OUP, 1982)
A generous sampling of translated poetry and prose (letters, laws, histories,
etc.) with brief introductions. Poems (including *Beowulf*) translated by
the editor, prose translations from various sources.

Daily Life in Anglo-Saxon England Sally Crawford (Greenwood, 2009)
Enjoyable account of the Anglo-Saxons as people: work, leisure, customs,
beliefs, etc.

Anglo-Saxon England Frank Stenton (Oxford U. Press, 1971)
A thorough history of the period, scholarly but readable.

The English Settlements J.N.L. Myres (Oxford U. Press, 1986)
The earliest days of Anglo-Saxon England, including archeological evidence.

The Oral Tradition

The Singer of Tales Albert Lord (Harvard U. Press, 1960)
Groundbreaking study of the techniques of oral epic composition, elabo-
rated in his other books below.

Epic Singers and Oral Tradition Albert Lord (Cornell U. Press, 1991)

The Singer Resumes the Tale Albert Lord, edited by Mary Louise Lord (Cornell
U. Press, 1995)
Posthumous collection of essays, edited by the author's wife.

Fiction

Grendel John Gardner (Knopf, 1971)
The Beowulf story as told by Grendel. This "monster's view" of human so-
ciety is the vehicle for all sorts of philosophical and ethical speculations.
One of the most inventive creations of a master storyteller.

Eaters of the Dead Michael Crichton (Knopf, 1976)
Reissued as *The Thirteenth Warrior* after the film: see below
An eyewitness account of the Vikings by Arab traveler ibn Fadlan serves as

the point of departure. Crichton posits that Grendel's mother (an enormous Venus of Willendorf) was queen of a primitive tribe of cannibals.

Films and Media

Beowulf: Benjamin Bagby, Voice and Anglo-Saxon Harp (Charles Murrow Productions LLC, 2006)
Benjamin Bagby gives a compelling performance of *Beowulf* in the original Anglo-Saxon (with subtitles), with a reconstructed Anglo-Saxon harp. Surprisingly entertaining, and perhaps as close as we'll ever come to hearing an Anglo-Saxon *scop*.

Beowulf (Robert Zemeckis, director. Paramount Home Entertainment, 2007)
Done in cartoon-like motion capture technique, this popular film features impressive special effects, especially for the dragon. The plot is "improved" by making Grendel the son of Hrothgar and a seductive demon played by Angelina Jolie.

Beowulf and the Anglo-Saxons (ARTSMAGIC, 2007)
This 90-minute video features readings in Anglo-Saxon, the Sutton Hoo ship burial, and the recreated Anglo-Saxon village at West Stow. Not a "neutral" educational video—like good Anglo-Saxons, these scholars have axes to grind. But their theories are interesting: *Beowulf*'s possible connection to a Geat/Wulfing kingdom in East Anglia, and Grendel's mother to an ancient fertility goddess.

Beowulf & Grendel (Grendel Productions Inc., 2005)
In this TV-quality production, Grendel and his mother are called "trolls," but seem to be simply human outcasts. Beowulf's love interest is a sorceress whose sympathies are divided between him and the "monsters."

The Thirteenth Warrior (Touchstone Home Entertainment, 2000)
Based on Michael Crichton's *Eaters of the Dead* (see above). Antonio Banderas is likeable as ibn Fadlan, a cultured Arab who learns heroism from the Viking barbarians. But the attempt to provide a "realistic" explanation for the monsters falls flat.